CW01426072

CHARLES

INSIDE THE HEART OF THE BIKINI KILLER

SOBHRAJ

400

CHARLES

INSIDE THE HEART OF THE BIKINI KILLER

SOBHRAJ

RAAMESH KOIRALA

RUPA

Published by
Rupa Publications India Pvt. Ltd 2018
7/16, Ansari Road, Daryaganj
New Delhi 110002

Sales centres:
Allahabad Bengaluru Chennai
Hyderabad Jaipur Kathmandu
Kolkata Mumbai

Copyright © Raamesh Koirala 2018

ISBN: 978-93-5333-262-4

First impression 2018

10 9 8 7 6 5 4 3 2 1

Printed at Parksons Graphics Pvt. Ltd., Mumbai

In 2003, there were nearly 190 countries in the world. Only one country had active cases of murder against Charles Sobhraj. He was free; he was a celebrity. He was believed to be making a hefty sum of money from interviews and photo sessions. Why on earth did he come to Nepal to find himself behind bars?

I was a doctor trying to fix his ailing heart. But I was consumed by the question.

I had to find the answer.

अक्षराणामकारोऽस्मिद्वन्द्वः सामासिकस्चय
अहमेवाक्षयः कालोधताहंविश्वतोमुखः ।।33।।

I am the beginning 'A' amongst all letters; I am the dual word in grammatical compounds. I am the endless Time, and amongst creators I am Brahma.

—(Bhagavad Gita, chapter 10, verse 33)

CONTENTS

PROLOGUE

'Sir, I will make the skin incision.'
'And I will cut his sternum.'

The two young doctors—Subita and Ansu—rattled off their wish-list in a single breath. It seemed like a pledge. Or a demand. I cannot say what exactly it was. I was used to seeing these young doctors giggling and gossiping every day, always as cheerful and excitable as schoolgirls. Their conversations usually seemed merry, far away from thoughts of dusty Kathmandu or its political system. Neither of them had even bothered to register their names in the voter list for the recent local election.

And yet, all of a sudden, they were making demands like these. No giggles. No smiles. Just a final, unchangeable decision.

They looked at me with solemn faces, determination writ large in their eyes. After a moment's consideration, I nodded, and pretended to get back to my papers. From the corner of my eyes, I could see their excitement—the excitement to cut open Charles Sobhraj's chest.

Subita and Ansu had been working at the hospital for a

year. They had made up their minds to resign before something happened to change the course of their lives. It wasn't unusual in the medical community for young doctors to take time off for postgraduate entrance examinations. But both of them had postponed their plans for one reason—to witness the surgery that would fix Charles Sobhraj's heart.

Now, not only were they getting a chance to witness the surgery but they would be an integral part of it. They would see his heart beating, almost human and yet not quite.

I was beginning to understand their excitement.

✶

'Hey! Did you know I am repairing Charles Sobhraj's valves?' I was back home and called out to Poonam, my wife. She was in the kitchen, marinating a chicken for dinner.

Poonam is a doctor herself and is always very interested to hear about the cases I pursue. But today, she did not answer.

Perhaps she hadn't heard me.

'I am fixing Charles Sobhraj's heart,' I repeated.

She turned around to look at me. There was no excitement on her face, no happiness for the challenging case her husband had been entrusted with. It was most unusual.

'Okay,' she said.

It dawned upon me at that moment—the reason for her cold, almost scared response.

Poonam's father had been a junior police officer at Tihar Jail in India—the jail from where Charles Sobhraj had escaped several years ago. Although Poonam had then been a little girl, she had watched her father fret every night, consumed by anxiety and unable to sleep. And now her husband was talking about the same notorious man—Charles Sobhraj.

My wife spent the next couple of hours locked up in her room. From the sound coming through the door, I could guess what she was up to. She was watching YouTube documentaries on Charles. She wanted to find out all she could about the con man, the cold-blooded murderer who had brought untold trauma to her father and had now sprung up in her husband's life.

During dinner that night, I tried to read her emotions. It was a quiet and tense meal; Poonam's mobile phone was lying next to her plate, overheated from streaming one video after another. I could still see a film by National Geographic on the screen, paused midway.

My wife met my eyes, voicing a question I had no idea how to answer.

'Does he even *have* a heart?'

1

PHONE DANDA:
A TELEPHONE RINGS

Saturday, 20 May 2017. It was early in the morning in far-western Nepal. Spring had been late that year. The constant sound of leaves crackling under our feet was the lone intruder in the calm of that humid morning. We were a group of six men in the temperate forest of Khaptad National Park, trekking along for all we were worth—panting like there'd be no tomorrow.

It was the picture-postcards that had got us excited about this adventure trip—the glorious subalpine meadows of the Khaptad Patan, grazing cows and goats, green carpets of grasslands dotted with tiny bukiphool,[1] impish little streams bisecting the famous Khaptad Baba's ashram. Who would not be inspired by these wonders?

---

[1] Subalpine wildflowers

We had been trekking for only a couple of hours, but it already seemed like an eternity. With every yard that we completed, the crackling of the leaves diminished. It was a herculean task to move, let alone climb.

I was beginning to think this had been an ill-considered idea, a foolish adrenaline rush for a few lazy bones from Kathmandu who had no preparation whatsoever. No physical training.

Let me introduce you to our group of amateur—but very enthused—trekkers. It was quite varied in membership.

There was Rameshworji aka Comrade, an established businessman who ran a security service company in Kathmandu. A devout foodie by heart, his focus since the beginning of the trip had been to taste the most bizarre items at the famous dhabas.

Then there was Anil, a fellow heart surgeon at my hospital who was always ready to trek. I think god had forgotten to add a neutral gear to his soul; he was always in the seventh heaven of excitement or down in the deepest pit of despair. But trekking never failed to get him spirited. He had shown me a perpetually-packed rucksack that he kept in the corner of his room. Talking to him always increased my inferiority complex for not travelling as much as I'd have liked, for being a frog in the well of familiar Kathmandu.

Next up was Subhash, an entrepreneur according to his Twitter bio. But for us, good old Subry was a born politician. He was deeply involved with the Nepali Congress Party (NCP), a social democratic party of Nepal. Interestingly, he was also an architect, industrialist, builder and philanthropist. After spending a decade in the United Kingdom, he had returned home for good to pursue all these interests. Well, life is too short just to do one thing, eh?

Pramod, an engineer and expert on road construction, was

the brains of the group. Truth be told, he was an expert on several subjects, much like an encyclopedia. But he knew how to have fun and get along with people.

And finally, there was Prakash, aka Babaji. He was a complete package of entertainment. Trekking was 'in his blood', and so was music; he could play all kinds of percussion instruments and sing any song in six different folksy rhythms. His artistic talents got magnified after a few glasses of alcohol. Prakash's pet peeve was a criticism of non-governmental organizations. He could not stand it if someone insulted NGOs and claimed that they were less interested in social upliftment and more in minting money. Babaji then went insane and launched into a full-blown attack, complete with statistics and emphatic slogans.

Did you notice how not a single member of the group had any significant trekking experience? The only thing we had was the desire to experience the beauty of Khaptad Patan. This heady desire had propelled us to trek 1,400 metres above the sea level from Kathmandu, descending to Attaria and ascending yet again to Jhingrana and beyond.

At Jhingrana, a small hamlet, our hotelier had shown us the sole peak we would need to conquer. Beyond that, he had assured us—and we had happily believed—there'd be a plateau. But his assurance had been illusory. Even after two terribly stiff hours of climbing, we were nowhere. That 'sole' peak was already under our feet, but we were staring at another, a taller one at that.

'Dai, let's offload Comrade's back pack some more,' Anil called out. I could see him and Rameshworji about 40 feet below. Anil was removing water bottles and packets of food from Comrade's camouflaged rucksack and transferring them to his bag. Even though Comrade was a first-time trekker, he had been the most excited about the plan. Presently, he stood breathing in alarming, wispy gusts. His face was deep red, sweat trickling down his brow.

I ran down quickly. 'Hey, Comrade! Are you okay?'

Comrade smiled back at me. Anil chuckled. Pretty soon, all of us were laughing heartily. Comrade's army bag rested jauntily on the ground, pretending it didn't mind being the object of our laughter.

For two whole days before the trek, Comrade had *very* diligently prepared his backpack. We had witnessed his preparation. In had gone two litres of Glenfiddich whisky, a one-litre water bottle filled to the brim, a heavy jacket, five pairs of clothing, three power banks, toiletries, and—wait for it—a laptop. Why would he ever need a computer in the thick of a jungle, atop a mountain peak? Why, to transfer pictures and videos from his two mobile phones, of course. He had even generously volunteered to carry two cans of beer for me. By the end, the bag, which weighed at least five kilograms by itself, was as suitable for a trekker as a bread knife is for a surgeon.

Between chuckles, we offloaded Comrade's bag. Anil moved the laptop, power banks and Glenfiddich to his rucksack. I took on some of the clothes and toiletries.

'Let's move on now,' I said, a little worried about the swiftly advancing day. I didn't particularly want to be in the middle of nowhere when night fell. 'We seem to have a few more peaks to climb before the plains.'

'How much more to climb?' asked Comrade, trying hard to sound relaxed but failing miserably. He was probably thinking about warm, delicious soup down at Jhingrana Hotel. If there had been network reception in our phones or a single soul in sight, I am sure he would have scooted. But let alone a porter or hotelier, there wasn't even a mule to be seen.

'They said four hours uphill and then three hours on the plain. Comrade, we are more than half of that uphill already.'

'You need this?' Anil enquired, holding a bamboo stick he had ferreted from a nearby bush. Comrade looked at it doubtfully—would clutching it make him a loser? He definitely did not want that. A Nepalese man with the ambition to cross the Thorangla Pass, 5,416 metres, next season could not be out of breath at only 3,000.

So, he trudged on bravely.

He trudged on bravely, demanding a break after every twenty steps.

I couldn't blame him; I too was finding it difficult to ascend. Our stock of drinking water was over, and we were relying on water from natural springs treated with two drops of chlorine.

'Wow, this bag is really evil!' called out Anil, who was now carrying the infamous army bag and looking much the worse for it. 'These plates and bottles keep nudging my back.'

Anil sat down, the bag off his back, and nursed the redness in his shoulder blades. We tried to adjust the straps but in vain.

'Let's carry that dratted bag in turns,' suggested Subhash. And that's what we did. If nothing else, we could at least share the back pain and redness. Those who share not only your happiness but also your pain are real friends. And we, amateur but determined trekkers, wanted to prove that!

Finally, after almost five hours of climbing, we reached Bichpani. It was a stop between Jhingrana and Khaptad and had a small hotel. As expected, there was no hotelier around. We stretched our legs, puffed a couple of cigarettes, and relaxed over a meal—if you could call it that.

'These dry noodles sure are yum.' Anil scowled as he chewed

on the noodles, interspersed with long swigs of tap water.

We moved on from Bichpani after about an hour and soon reached the jungle. The trails were not that steep anymore, but our bodies could do little more than drag along. After every five metres, we sat down to rest and nibbled on biscuits. Pretty soon, we finished our last packet of biscuits.

'All we now have to eat is jungle fruit. And animal meat.' I said, suddenly ravenous for that soup I had chided Comrade for dreaming about.

'What animals? Apart from birdsong and mule excreta, I cannot see any sign of animals,' Anil sneered.

'Oh no, look at those diggings near the bamboo roots,' said Comrade, conspiratorially. 'In my trekker's books, I read that wild boars have a habit of doing that.'

'Brilliant,' Anil clapped. 'In our 22-kilometre stretch, we are only halfway through, and it has already been seven hours. That was the time they said it would take to go from Jhingrana to Khaptad! We've only had sickly noodles and biscuits to eat, and now boars are lying in wait!'

Things sure looked bleak. Comrade, Pramod and I were feeling extremely frail though we didn't want to abandon the trek. Subhash, Prakash and Anil were about to leave. I didn't mind. I was getting tired of Anil's sneering and complaining. Plus, we wouldn't have to carry that evil army bag anymore!

It was then that I jumped out of my skin. I think everyone did.

All our mobile phones were ringing. All six of them, the ringtones loud and menacing in the deathly silence of the forest.

We were in the midst of a jungle, halfway to Khaptad. There was no visible mobile tower. We hadn't had any connectivity for several hours now. And yet, suddenly, more than half of the little network lines in my phone were lit.

My call was from Gyanmani Mama, my maternal uncle.

'Mama! *Dhog*,' I said, using the Nepali expression for showing respect. 'What's up?'

'Can I come to you? It's something urgent.'

'Why not? Please come.'

Subhash, who had already finished his call—goodness knows from whom—was now laughing at me. Mama's call had caught me so unaware that I was inviting him to join me in the address-less wilderness.

'Where are you? At the hospital? Can I come right away?'

'Mama, get a chopper and come here. I'm nearby. A few kilometres from Bichpani.'

'Where?'

He didn't get me. Obviously. He was planning to visit me at the familiar hospital, and here I was, talking about choppers and strange places. Knowing mama, he was probably hearing about Bichpani for the first time in his life.

'Mama, I am walking to Khaptad with some friends. Is there anything serious?'

'Yes. When will you come back?'

I calculated quickly. It was Saturday. If everything went as planned, we would be back in Kathmandu by Wednesday evening.

'Wednesday,' I told mama. 'What is the matter?'

I thought I heard him take a deep breath before responding, 'Do you know Charles Sobhraj?'

Did I know him! A few weeks ago, I had met him in my outpatient chamber at Shahid Gangalal Hospital. He was fair-complexioned and wore a Lenin-type beret. Our cardiologist had referred him here, and one of my colleagues was going through his reports. Naturally, his reputation preceded him, and I was gripped despite myself. I had even clicked a snap of the 'Bikini Killer' after taking his permission—something I was not proud of. How could I forget that meeting? It had been my personal 'Encounter with a Convict'—an English fictitious essay I had once written in school.

'Charles Sobhraj!' I blurted out loudly, forgetting that curious ears were tuned to my conversation. I continued in a hushed tone, 'Yes, I do know him. He is supposed to get admitted for surgery, right?'

It was a high-profile case, one that everyone in the hospital had been animatedly discussing for weeks. Navin, my fellow surgeon, had a plan to admit Charles Sobhraj for surgery. He wanted to repair his heart valves after coronary angiography, a procedure to check the vessels supplying blood to the heart muscles. I thought Charles was already in the hospital.

'Bhanja,[2] we want you to be present in that surgery. Is it possible?'

'We? Who? And why are *you* asking this?' I could not imagine any possible connection between Charles Sobhraj and my uncle. Charles, a serial killer, was in Kathmandu at a time mama had not even crossed the Koshi River in eastern Nepal. In 2003, when Charles was arrested in Kathmandu, it had been as huge a surprise for him as most other Nepalese people. I could not connect the dots. And now, this 'we'—what was that about?

'Shakuntala Didi wants to talk to you.' Ah, here it was.

Shakuntala was Charles's lawyer. I could recall her face from the television news in 2010; she had made headlines for criticising the court's verdict on Charles Sobhraj. Promptly, they

---

[2]Sister's son

had arrested her for contempt of court.

I was in no mood to talk to her. Certainly not when I was on a leisure trip, even though it was hardly leisurely to walk 22 kilometres in one day without food and water.

'Navin is a good surgeon, and things will be fine, mama. Tell Shakuntalaji to relax.' I desperately wanted to wrap up the conversation. It was making me distinctly uneasy.

'We will wait,' he said.

Without further delay, I said, 'Okay,' and disconnected the call.

Even before I had looked up from the mobile screen, I knew five pairs of eyes were staring at me.

★

I was right. All my fellow trekkers were looking at me unblinkingly, bursting with curiosity. Comrade was the last one to stop fiddling with his mobile phone.

'What's going on?' They questioned in unison. 'What's this about Charles Sobhraj?'

Ah, I loved it when my friends were consumed with curiosity. I might as well have some fun at their expense. A few more minutes of anticipation never killed anyone.

'So, who were your calls from?' I asked.

Anil made a face. 'Nothing much. It was just my wife checking to see if the mountains had eaten me up yet. Ditto for Prakash.'

I laughed. 'And what about you, Comrade?'

'I gave a good yelling to that army officer who gave me this dratted rucksack. Told him what I think of people who spoil others' plans.'

Comrade seemed inclined to go on for a while about the

woes of the wrong bag. Anil cut him short. 'To enlighten you
on the rest of the *critical* information: Subhash just got updated
on the vote-counting in the Tokha municipality. Pramod heard
from a road contractor on a frightfully important matter and
checked on his daughter's karate class. Now you go!'

'Oh, that reminds me. I need to call home too.' I quickly
dialled Poonam's number; thankfully, my phone still had
network reception. Somehow, I was unsure when I'd get another
chance to check on her.

'Will you please tell us now?' said Prakash. 'Or do you want
to bask in the attention some more?'

'I will. But I must have something to drink first. Comrade,
is there anything in your dukaan[3]?' I nodded towards his bag.
We had run out of water, but perhaps there was a saviour in
some crevice of that giant bag?

Comrade rummaged through the contents and magically
brought out a 200-ml tetrapack of mango juice. I sipped the
deliciously sweet mango drink and began to tell them the story—
the story of Charles Sobhraj.

★

'It was Gyanmani Mama on the phone,' I began. 'He was talking
about Charles Sobhraj. You know, the serial killer?'

I find the term 'serial killer' very interesting. It is menacing,
yes, but it doesn't give anything away. Was the murderer seeking
revenge? Was he or she insane? Were the people he or she killed
connected in any way?

'His deeds are infamous all over the world—all the way to
Paris. But strangely, in the mid '70s, he turned up in Kathmandu.

---

[3]Hindi word for shop

He killed several Westerners. You must have heard about him; it was all over the news. The man even managed to escape from Tihar Jail, the toughest prison in India.'

I looked around at my listeners; they all seemed perplexed. Why was I talking about serial killers? Why indeed? I decided to change the subject.

'So, how is your Sandhya ma'am doing?' I grinned at Subhash. We all knew about his special interest in Sandhya and her performance in the ongoing local-level election. He was keen that this well-educated and deserving candidate be crowned the sub-mayor of his municipality.

'Don't change the subject,' said Subhash, looking as if he wanted to talk about her nonetheless. 'She is still 300 votes behind. But you know, she will make it when the ballot boxes from our ward are opened.' Subhash was an active cadre of the Nepali Congress Party, a political party founded by Bishweshwor Prasad Koirala who was a close friend of renowned socialists like Ram Manohar Lohia and Jai Prakash Narayan. His party had managed to overthrow the Rana regime from Nepal. But the genuineness of the socialism it practised remained open for debate in Nepal, much like the operations of the Indian National Congress and the various offshoots of the Janata Dal in India.

'Will you *please* tell us about your call?' Anil sounded pained. Patience had never been his forte. Plus, a popularity contest between a sincere female politician and a notorious murderer is unreasonably one-sided.

'There's nothing much to tell. Charles Sobhraj has leaking heart valves and needs to undergo surgery. It was scheduled for tomorrow, I think, but they have postponed it.'

'Why?'

'I am not sure. Navin was supposed to operate, but it seems Charles and his family members are keen to...um...have me lead the surgery instead.' I made a rather half-hearted attempt to sound modest.

'So, what have you decided?' Comrade asked, fascinated.

'I will see when I get back.'

'Have you met him? How does he look?' Comrade sat up straight this time, clearing his throat for more questions.

'Let's talk while we walk, okay? We need to get going.'

Our little party set off again, led by—most surprisingly— Comrade! Suddenly, he wasn't slow anymore. He didn't even get out of breath too often.

'So, tell me more about this Charles person. Whom did he kill? What was the motive?'

'I have heard he killed many hippie girls after raping them, the bastard,' Subry announced. From his response, I couldn't guess what he wanted to emphasize more—the murder or the rape. Or maybe it was just the hatred he had for the Bikini Killer.

'Sa personnalité used to seduce women to death!' Anil tried, rather poorly, to imitate a French accent.

Comrade was intrigued. 'How did you know about his accent, doctor saab?' I wondered what it was about Charles's story that had reinvigorated our exhausted friend. Perhaps it was the nature of his business; maybe he wanted to learn the tricks this suave man used to defeat prison-grade security.

'I watched *Main Aur Charles* back in 2015.' Anil was an avid movie lover.

'But Taran Adarsh gave it a dismal rating,' pointed out Pramod, an avid Bollywood lover. 'Was it any good?'

★

Now, Charles was the prime subject of our conversation. We trudged along the terrain, my legs longing for a rest. But Comrade was coping exceedingly well. There was a spring in his steps I hadn't seen before, and he was the last one to agree to breaks. Subhash and Anil kept up a steady stream of gossip about Charles, a lot of it undoubtedly engineered. For the first time, I started feeling happy about that phone call. Gyanmani Mama truly cared about his bhanja.

Finally, after seemingly interminable hours, we arrived at Khaptad Patan.

I looked around. A lonely cottage lay in wait for us, with four dirty rooms and waterless toilets. Waterless, smelly toilets. Or perhaps the smell came from us; we had taken shelter in a cowshed to avoid being soaked—and beaten—by a sudden hailstorm. I longed to take a shower, change into fresh, dry clothes, and sit down for a hearty meal.

'Dinner is ready, saab!' The hotelier beamed at us and presented the wholesome menu—rice, noodles, lentil soup and black tea. Our faces must have fallen several inches, for he generously offered to roast some potatoes too.

In about an hour, we were sitting around a table in the twilight, finishing our meal and drinking beer. It was a cold night, rapidly getting colder. Comrade had fallen silent. Perhaps he missed the Jhingrana Hotel where he would sit by the fire, stirring local kukhura—a particularly delicious chicken. During our stay there, Comrade had acquired a whole rooster for ₹2,500. He had barbecued it lovingly, narrating endless gastronomic tales. The aroma of the kukhura had been so tempting that Comrade had ended up eating several charred pieces directly from the burning coal.

Prakash was quiet too. Of course, his reason for missing

Jhingrana was not remotely as innocent.

I remembered the morning from two days ago, when we had arrived at the hotel—Khaptad Sandesh Hotel and Lodge, Jhingrana. As soon as I had offloaded our truck, Prakash called out to me.

'Sir, come here. Look at this!'

I looked where he pointed. A green field, measuring about ten by six feet, lay behind a small hut. The field was flourishing; the crop was already taller than me and had grown into its distinctive, serrated form. It was a field full of weed.

'You want some now?' Last year, I had seen him high on marijuana during our camping trip to the Marsyangdi River in Lamjung. He went to great lengths to acquire a steady stock of weed—a pursuit that wasn't straightforward in Nepal. And here, the hotelier himself had the good stuff for Babaji to savour.

'Ask him. I am sure he won't mind.'

Just then, someone tugged at my shirt sleeve from behind. It was one of the kids who had been following us ever since we stepped down at Jhingrana. The boy couldn't have been older than ten, but his face was already hard and weather-beaten. In his right hand, he tightly clutched a dragonfly. 'Dai! Give us a hundred rupees!'

'No,' I said firmly. I detested Kathmandu's 'one dollar please!' practice of begging and had no intention of encouraging it here. The kids went away, scowling and calling us names.

By the evening, I knew the complete story of our hotelier, Mr Prem Bahadur Saud. He was a stooping, rather ill-tempered man in his late sixties. His wife Pampha Devi, whom I had embarrassingly mistaken for his daughter, was a charming lady in her early twenties. Through the day, she competently managed an array of tasks—killing mosquitoes, stirring the curry, and wiping her daughter's runny nose (not in that order). She had married Mr Saud after his first wife passed away. The couple moved to Jhingrana from Bajhang to distance themselves from a family dispute and start a new life together. Money was good—even though he had to pay 20,000 rupees to the landlord and spend about 70,000 for the upkeep of the hotel, the 'cash crop' made up for everything. For more than everything.

Babaji had made the most of the cash crop during our stay in Jhingrana. He had meticulously removed the tobacco from his cigarettes and replaced it with something, well, warmer.

At Khaptad on that cold night, how could he not miss the familiar, intoxicating warmth?

★

The next morning was a little warmer, no hailstorm in sight. Comrade looked rejuvenated after the rest. But he still didn't have the energy or the disposition to walk back to Jhingrana. We teased him and complained, but I, for one, was secretly thrilled. Memories of the day before—our gruelling trek without food and water—were vivid in my mind. We spent the morning sightseeing in Khaptad and discussing options for our return. Unless we found a motorable road, it would have to be a chopper.

The entire day, Charles was with us. He breakfasted with us, lingering in our conversations, and walked alongside, unseen, when we went to visit Khaptad Baba's ashram. He sulked when we went back to the hotel, late in the evening, for dinner now dominated our conversation. We had bought a local goat and Comrade was narrating in depth how he would barbecue it, serving roasted pieces as a snack and pairing it with Masu-bhat[4]

---

[4]A rice dish popular in Nepal

for a complete meal. The narration was delicious, and all of us listened hungrily.

En route to our hotel, we came across an army barrack. It lay isolated and silent but filled our hearts with audible delight. 'Army camps have mules!' Anil voiced what all of us were thinking.

'Care to see if the army guys want to join us for a drink?' I asked the group. 'And perhaps share some of their mules in return?'

Inside the barrack, the in-charge was Major Banskota. He sat listening to music, his eyes closed, and didn't register our presence until I cleared my throat. Comrade didn't lose any time in inviting him for a chat over Glenfiddich; he didn't lose any in accepting the invitation.

'We visited Khaptad Baba's ashram today,' I said, hoping to pique the Major's interest. 'I have heard he was actually Subhas Chandra Bose.'

'No, he wasn't,' The Major retorted instantly. 'He was a doctor from Kashmir. He left his home in the early fifties and came here. He practised meditation and cured local cattlemen of their ailments using only natural herbs. His knowledge of the medicinal herbs in the subalpine area was exceptional.'

'Then what's with this rumour about him being Netaji?' Subhas asked him.

'Complete nonsense. Khaptad Baba was a true sanyasi. His real name was Sri Paramahansa Satchidananda Saraswati. Baba had close ties with our royal family. He died here a couple of years before the Nepalese royal massacre.'

The Major seemed to know quite a lot about Khaptad Baba and proceeded to enlighten us about his life and times. I regretted bringing up the subject. Much as I had admired the picturesque ashram that morning, I seriously disbelieved the tale of a magical doctor residing in this barren grassland, meditating for decades.

But the Major evidently had no such reservations. He put on an enamoured expression and recited a poem:

Oh, Khaptad!
You take my breath away!
I am gasping for air.
Please fill my lungs…
…with the breeze touching the meadow.
Oh, Khaptad!
You're heaven on earth.

It turned out, Major was a 'budding poet' or maybe the magical splendour of Khaptad was the culprit. He had published a few poems online and had even been featured in *Seti Darpan*, a local newspaper. Fuelled by his love for Khaptad—and also by that second bottle of single malt—Major regaled us with poetry. I am rather dense about poetry, but what I heard that evening can only be described as true-blue torture. Army grade.

Three good things came out of that evening. First, we managed to arrange mules to return to Bichpani. Second, the Major was kind enough to offer high-energy army biscuits and dry food for the road. And third, our knowledge of Khaptad Baba could now rival that of a historian.

★

Back at the hotel, no one even mentioned rice and goat soup for dinner, not even Comrade. Our stomachs were churning with all the biscuits and pegs of Glenfiddich. I remember seeing the moon stream in through the window as I fell asleep. It was a deep slumber, the one you get after miles of walking and hours of bad poetry.

Something woke me up at midnight. I could hear a strange sound over the hotel. It sounded like an aeroplane. I quickly put on a jacket and ran out of the room.

Outside, I couldn't see a thing. I distinctly remembered having fallen asleep to the soothing moonlight, but it was daylight already. Had the night been so short? The whirring noise was only getting louder, and I scanned the sky overhead. There it was. A Mitsubishi Ki-21, flying south. I made up my mind to trail the plane. Running as quickly as my tired feet could carry me, I followed the plane. I came down to where the army barrack should have been, except it wasn't. Startled, I looked back in the distance to where my hotel was. It wasn't there either. Everything had vanished into thin air.

Presently, I found myself in Ghode Patan—Horse Meadow— the largest meadow in Khaptad and the host of the annual horse race for neighbouring villages. The Major had told us all about the meadow the night before. What he hadn't told us, however, was that it was also a landing spot for aircraft. I was stunned to see, in front of me, the aeroplane I had been trailing. It had landed in the plains of Ghode Patan, its twin propellers swiftly decelerating. Now that I had a closer look, I saw the aeroplane was actually Sally—the plane Netaji had boarded before disappearing. I had seen the pictures in newspapers for weeks after his disappearance.

The door of the aeroplane opened. A man in an army uniform jumped out. He was wearing a pair of thick glasses. To my immense surprise, he waved at me. 'Hey!' he called out, before hurriedly climbing a nearby hillock and disappearing behind some trees.

I had barely composed myself when another man appeared from behind the trees. He was wearing saffron. He too waved at me. But wait, this man I knew.

'Babaji!' I screamed.

'What happened, Sir?' Babaji was standing in front of my bed, looking at me with surprise and concern. 'Did you have a nightmare?'

I was back in my room, far away from Ghode Patan, no aeroplane in sight. 'It was nothing,' I said, rubbing my eyes and pretending to be relaxed. At that moment, I was acutely aware of the cold sweat that had drenched my body.

I didn't know then what the dream signified. I was not a believer in the notion that dreams can foretell your future. And yet, after I got back in Kathmandu, the mystery man in my dream became my reality. The nightmare had been a warning.

*

We met Major saab again that day to coordinate the mule-transport. He was pleased to see us. 'I had such fun talking with you young men that evening. Did I tell you about the most loved peak in the Khaptad National Park?'

'No, which one is it?' Prakash enquired.

'It is in an isolated area, in the thick of the wilderness. But guess what, before Khaptad got its solar-powered mobile tower, that was the sole spot in the entire national park where you could get a mobile signal. All the infantrymen used to go down to that hillock to call their loved ones. That's how the peak got its name—Phone Danda.'

2

MY DOCTOR IS CLIMBING THE MOUNTAINS

I was back to my daily routine as a heart surgeon. For four days a week, I ran an outpatient clinic. For the remaining work week, I conducted surgeries. Thanks to my holiday to Khaptad, several cases had piled up. But I was not complaining—the trip had been memorable.

At lunchtime everyday, I recollected memories of my recent journey and shared my experiences with my fellow doctors. The green meadows at Khaptad, the blue water of the Karnali River, the excitement of it all. I conveniently concealed our trekking misadventures and the ample evidence our bodies had provided of being totally unsuited for physical exercise. I was a heart surgeon, wasn't I? So, I proudly displayed my sunburned arms—high-altitude trekking is notorious for the worst sunburn cases, particularly when you wear half-sleeved shirts.

'Wasn't it cold?' asked a colleague.

'Oh, not for me. Plus, you see, we trekkers often wear half-sleeved shirts to control sweat.'

★

In the coming week, the ICC Cricket Championship was set to start. I was eagerly waiting for it. I was rooting for India to win, primarily because of Mahendra Singh Dhoni. I will admit, I am quite an MS Dhoni fanboy, and became a fan of the Indian Cricket team mainly because of him. The recent news about Dhoni giving up his captaincy had dismayed me, but even so, it was thrilling to see him sail through as a batsman, scoring a thousand, five thousand, and then, ten thousand ODI runs!

I was thinking about him as I finished my routine duties at the hospital. It was Wednesday—my outpatient clinic day. I completed my rounds of the ICU and the wards by 11:30 a.m. and headed towards the OPD—room number 16.

I switched on the light in the corridor. In the waiting area, patients sat waiting for me, chatting with their friends and relatives. Some of them called out to me in greeting. I smiled at them and opened the door to my room.

And I saw him. Mr Hatchand Bhaonani Gurumukh Charles Sobhraj. The infamous con man, the serpentine murderer, now in his early seventies. He sat there inside my cabin, handcuffed, and surrounded by four policemen.

Even though Gyanmani Mama's phone call had alerted me to this upcoming meeting, I was not expecting to see him so early. I was clueless about how to react. Navin hadn't shown up yet, so I didn't have a chance to talk to him and pretend that I didn't see the policemen. Or the handcuffs.

I sat down on my chair and switched on the patient-call

machine. Charles Sobhraj hurried towards me almost as soon as I had pressed 1, 2 and 3.

'Hey, doctor! Can you help me?'

'Hello,' I said, quickly looking at one of the policemen. I was distinctly uneasy, seeing four burly, uniformed men in my clinic, all guarding my patient as if he could dash off any minute. 'Please sit down,' I pointed to the stool opposite my chair.

'Can you fix a meeting with my doctor? I think I need heart surgery.'

I tried to look nonchalant. I did not particularly want to divulge that I knew all about his ailment. Navin and I had discussed at length the specific type of surgery that Charles needed. It had been all we had talked about ever since we first got the news. Moreover, I could guess where this conversation was headed.

'I think Dr Navin was supposed to operate on you. What happened?' I wanted to play a purely defensive game, just like Rahul Dravid batting in front of the wickets, extremely conscious of Shane Warne's bowling.

'Not him. Can you fix a meeting with *my* doctor?'

'Who is your doctor?' I persisted. As an MS Dhoni fan, I was ready for the helicopter shot, if only I was offered a relatively loose ball.

'I heard that my doctor is climbing the mountains.'

Mountains? Really? Even though I had once gone to the Annapurna base camp and had recently returned from a subalpine meadow, I was no mountaineer. 'Who?'

'They told me Dr Koirala had taken an off for climbing.'

Ah, there were two Dr Koiralas in the hospital. I jumped at the chance to hit his off-stump Yorker. 'Which Koirala?'

'No, no, not that one.' For someone new to the hospital,

he seemed uncannily aware of all its doctors. 'I want Dr Ramis Koirala from Gangalal.'

Oh, god.

'I'm *Raamesh* Koirala. Is it me you are looking for?'

His facial expression changed; his jaw dropped visibly. He probably remembered me from one of his old visits. There was that time when he had even allowed me to click a picture. He had probably put me down as a member of the paparazzi.

For a few seconds, he didn't say a word. I enjoyed those seconds tremendously.

'Aaare... Are you the Dr Ramis Koirala?'

It is *Raamesh*, I wanted to pinpoint again. I hated it when people mispronounced my name. Early in my marriage, I had even given a piece of my mind to Poonam, elaborating upon the difference between 'Ramesh', a name that refers to Lord Vishnu, and 'Raamesh', a rather not-so-common name which refers to Lord Shiva. But I must admit, the article before my name—almost like The King of Nepal VI—pacified me.

'I was visiting Khaptad, not mountaineering.'

'Doctor saab, he wants you to correct him the operation,' one of the policemen—an assistant sub-inspector—stepped forward. 'We had to take him back last week.'

Normally, I didn't take too long to decide the cases I wanted to handle. Previously too, I had been approached by friends and relatives of my ex-patients, people who selected surgeons based on recommendations, much like the movies they watched. But this time, it wasn't that straightforward to say yes. I knew I had to review many aspects first. Would I be able to reschedule my operating list? Or would I need to operate him on overtime? I needed to talk to Navin—his surgeon-in-charge—about this swapping. I also had to check with the hospital administration on the procedural requirements of admitting a convict of such monstrous reputation from the Central Jail.

But most importantly, I had to convince myself that I was steely enough to operate on a cold-blooded killer. For all my medical experience, this was something I had never done!

I found myself unable to decide. As a doctor, it was my moral—and professional—responsibility to attend to my patients, even if their occupation was murdering people. But that morning, reluctance prevailed. I looked at my medical officer, Sabita. Her face was blank.

'Let's meet another day.'

★

'Doctor Raamesh! A Shakuntala Thapa is on the phone. What should I say?'

It was the morning after my meeting with Charles. I was in the operation theatre when Sushila, my OT nurse, called out to me.

On my operating days, I usually put my phone on a nearby tray. I instructed someone from the team to answer it. 'Is it anything urgent?'

I heard Sushila talk on the phone for a minute. 'She is asking for a good time to talk to you today.'

'Tell her to call after two hours.'

I knew I would be able to finish the ongoing surgery—a little kid with Tetralogy of Fallot, a congenital heart condition—in an hour. But I wanted to buy myself time.

★

Breakfast was usually a rushed meal for me. My mind was always preoccupied with the tasks of the day. I sat at the table, speedily working through my toast, when my mobile phone vibrated. A number beginning with 980 was flashing on the screen.

I instantly put down my bread and stared. Numbers beginning with 980 or 981 angered me. For more than a year now, I hadn't been answering calls from such numbers to protest against the mobile network provider NCell. The ownership of NCell was set to be transferred from TeliaSonera to Axiata, a Malaysian company, and the deal was decidedly murky. People in the know-how claimed that NCell was depriving our country of capital gain tax worth nearly 50 billion Nepalese rupees. The money that was ours by right was being surreptitiously transferred to an offshore hoax company in Virgin Islands. On my weekly off, I spent considerable time campaigning on social media against the deal. Subhash and I had even given public statements on the matter in a feature on Swedish television. And suddenly, my public vow not to answer any call from NCell was being challenged.

I still don't know why I picked up.

'Hello, Raamesh here.'

'Doctor saab, this is Shakuntala. Gyanmani Babu must have told you about me.'

I knew I should have stuck to my resolution against NCell. While I had never met—or talked to—Shakuntala before, I felt as if I knew her quite well. The media loved talking about her life. No wonder that, considering she was not only Charles's lawyer but also allegedly his mother-in-law. Over the years, one dramatized television programme after another had portrayed how Charles and Nihita Biswas, Shakuntala's daughter, had fallen in love. Nihita, claimed the programmes, had progressed from being his French interpreter to the love of his life. One Dashain morning—the Nepalese version of Durga Puja—she pledged to make him 'her man'. Although only a young girl in her early twenties, Nihita had already reached thousands of households through the prime-time television show *Bigg Boss*. The blockbuster Indian reality show was almost as huge a hit in Nepal. I remember guffawing when she had been invited for *Bigg Boss*, although I am not sure why.

'Doctor saab, are you there?'

I feigned a cough. 'Yes, Gyanmani Mama told me about you. What's up?'

'Please do the surgery!' she insisted, coming straight to the point. 'He wants to be operated only by you, Bhanja!'

Wait, bhanja? I guess she was trying to copy Gyanmani Mama's relation with me. My mother just became Shakuntala's elder sister! What an instant addition to the family, almost like the two-minute Maggi noodles. However 'bhanja' is reserved to mama and maiju, mother's sister-in-law. A strange relation was brewing up!

'Okay, Didi, let me be honest with you. Why should I have to operate on a serial killer? Only to get condemned?' I stuck to calling her didi, or sister. Calling her sanima, or my mother's sister, was too much. It was too intimate, too personal.

'We have searched a lot for a good surgeon, trust me. We even filed a plea for his release so he could get operated in France.'

I remembered seeing a tweet about this by the Indian actor, Randeep Hooda. He had played the character of Charles in the movie, *Main Aur Charles*. Randeep had posted a plea on his social media page, urging the Nepalese government to allow Charles to go to France for his heart surgery. It wasn't safe for him in Nepal.

'So? What happened?'

'Nothing. Nothing is working for us.'

For almost twenty minutes, Shakuntala explained to me why Charles deserved my consideration. How he was innocent, how he was being subjected to extreme injustice. He was on his best behaviour in jail, she said, and there had never been any complaint against him. My patience was running thin. I wondered how she had the heart to tell me so many 'truths' about Charles except the fact that he was her son-in-law.

'Will you please see us tomorrow, then?'

'Okay,' I said and pressed the end-call button on my phone.

✶

The next day, my clinic was again full of policemen—five this time. I could not see Charles anywhere. Yakub, a paid agent of religious conversion and one of my old patients, was waiting too. I was about to motion to Yakub to come over when one of the policemen greeted me.

'Head Constable Raju, doctor saab. I have come with his lawyer.'

His lawyer could only mean one person. I saw an old lady in her sixties walk through the door, a small smile on her heavily-wrinkled face. Shakuntala Thapa.

'I am sorry for being late,' she said softly.

'No, I should be the one to apologize.' I had agreed to meet Shakuntala at 11:00 a.m. But that morning on my way to work, something horrible had delayed me. A microbus hit a young school teacher at Basundhara while she was crossing the road. She was at the zebra crossing, following the traffic rules. Only a month ago, the traffic police had introduced a penalty of ₹200 if pedestrians attempted to cross the road outside the zebra crossing. But, unfortunately, rules don't have a foolproof record of saving lives.

'It's no problem at all, Bhanja.'

I looked carefully at my 'new' maternal aunt. On an average day, I tend to stir up old memories with the patients in my outpatient clinic, endeavouring to make them feel comfortable. I was quite famous in the hospital for my great 'sense of déjà vu', second only to my colleague, Dr Mana Bahadur. Mana could draw your entire family tree even if you had been conceived in a test tube. But try as I did, I could not remember meeting Shakuntala before this.

She was short, a little frail, and spoke in a thin voice. She was nothing, I decided, like my 5.5-feet-tall mother with her authoritative voice that could alert the entire neighbourhood at once. 'This goat weighs 32 kilos and would be perfect for Dashain,' mum would announce, and bingo, the neighbourhood would set the going rate. There was no way this woman with her reedy voice could be my mother's sister. I had a sudden, intense desire to tell her bluntly: 'Please don't call me bhanja.' Somehow I suppressed the desire.

'Bhanja, we want an early surgery,' Shakuntala was saying.

I wondered if this had anything to do with Sobhraj's Supreme Court hearing; I had heard some gossip around it. How did Shakuntala feel about the upcoming hearing? Did she get nightmares about the verdict that would be passed? Her face with its glistening dark eyes did not give away much. She occasionally smiled—a smile incongruent with the anxiety I could sense in her voice. I could feel that morning what I had missed on the phone—this woman may be Charles's lawyer-in-charge, but she was his mother-in-law first.

'Today is not my OPD day. Moreover, I have just said yes to someone.' I gestured towards Yakub.

I thought she would be riled. That she would scream, 'I want you to see my client and fix a date as early as possible!'

But instead, she said quite gently, 'Would you please see him tomorrow?'

I nodded. 'See you on Tuesday.'

★

Subry was getting his pick-up truck, a brand new Toyota Hilux, ready. Our stay in Sauraha—one of the stops along the Khaptad trail—had been pleasant, and we were now planning our ride back to Kathmandu. I saw Subry struggling with a thread of some sort, seemingly wrapped around the back of the truck.

'What's up?'

'Some kid must have done this.' He sighed, throwing away the string with a small winged creature attached to its end. A dried carcase of a dragonfly.

I knew which kid had done that. Subry must have forgotten the ugliness of that evening, but I remembered every detail.

That evening, two kids had turned up at our hotel. I recognized them from the group of beggars who had begged us for a hundred rupees in Jhingrana, scowling fiercely when we refused. How could I forget the cruel look they had given us when a tête-à-tête with cruelty was imminent in my future?

We were sitting outside, sipping beer. One of the kids had a dragonfly—alive this time—in his right hand. He grinned at us and sat down on the muddy ground, brandishing his captive.

'Dai! Do you want to buy this?'

None of us paid him any attention. But he had a Plan B. He took out a small roll of thread from his pocket and knotted it around the dragonfly's tail. All of us were busy pretending he didn't exist, even though we couldn't help be a little intrigued.

The little monster then proceeded to run up and down the small dirt road, flinging about the thread with its rapidly suffocating dragonfly. 'Hu haaaa!' he squealed each time the poor creature tried to open its wings. But how could a defenceless dragonfly possibly escape the will of its cruel, laughing master?

'Let it be!' Pramod shouted. 'Enough is enough.'

'Then give me two hundred rupees. I will let it go.'

His price had doubled, much like that of taxi drivers in Kathmandu whenever it remotely looked like it was going to rain. On one overcast evening some months ago, I had quite an argument with a taxi driver about this unreasonable pricing. 'Sir, driving in a light intensity below 50 Lux burns petrol twofold,' he told me. Apparently, taxis need generators to illuminate the road ahead! It was a ludicrous argument. But the bargain that this kid was offering was devoid of even absurd logic—it was plainly, irrationally disgusting.

'Don't you dare blackmail us,' I told him. 'Off with you!'

The unstoppable kid paid no attention. He continued his devilish activity while we moved inside to the kitchen. Barbecuing local kukhura somehow seemed less cruel than watching that dragonfly meet its gruesome end.

How can children be so cruel? Do circumstances bring out the worst in people? I found myself ill at ease as Subry threw away the decapitated, wingless dragonfly. It had been hanging from the back of his truck for days.

★

'Taste the Jalkapur. It is divine!' Comrade was holding a rather nasty-smelling freshwater trout, encouraging me to eat it raw. We were at Benighat, en route to Sauraha once again. But this weekend, we were travelling without any grand trekking plans. Subry wanted to visit his new concrete brick factory—autoclaved and aerated—for probably the umpteenth time. My daughter Ishita had joined us for an elephant ride and jungle safari in the Chitwan National Park. She was excited about the rhinos waiting to greet her, and the deer she would click pictures with. Comrade was here for the duck and the fish. I, on the other hand, wanted to talk to my friends about the dilemma I was in.

'Should I operate on him?' I looked quizzically at Comrade and Subry. 'I cannot arrive at a decision.'

Comrade had been too engrossed inspecting the cans of mustard oil we had loaded in the truck to enhance the flavour of the roasted duck at Hari's Den. Along with beer by the poolside of the Landmark Hotel, the duck was a regular highlight of our visits to Chitwan. Comrade just looked at me distractedly.

'Is this all of the local kukhura we have left?' Subry asked Ishita. His question told me two things: One, our meal earlier that day—barbecued chicken—had failed to keep him full for long. And two, rooster meat was more important than any medical dilemma. I sighed audibly.

'I have already posted pictures of German and Russian embassies, as you wanted,' Comrade said to me without taking his eyes off his phone. He had recently signed up for a 4G network connection and was spiritedly using the new-found speed to express outrage against multiple issues. The lawlessness of public-vehicle drivers. Big embassies occupying the pavement. The unfairness meted out to pedestrians walking from Chakrapath to Maharajgunj, who now found a wall in the middle of the route. The US embassy, with its massive building and ample land, was in favour of the Geneva Convention but not the convenience of the local people. Neither were the German,

Japanese, French and Russian embassies. This scenario enraged Comrade and was at the top of his mental priority list. I wasn't even *on* the list.

'French is still missing,' I pointed out, giving up hope of getting any advice that day. I tried to focus instead on the hashtag, '#LetUsWalk', which, according to Comrade, was 'totally brilliant'.

My daughter switched seats with Comrade, seating herself at the corner to get a closer look at a fisherman. The lone man was sitting quietly, perhaps hoping to catch some Jalkapur. A few rafts and kayaks passed by. Ishita was an experienced rafter; she had already rafted thrice, screaming with increasing volume, depending on the grade of the rapids in the Trishuli River.

Subry drove on, sipping beer and giving two hoots to the 'no drunk driving' rule. Comrade was deeply occupied in liking all the tweets by his favourite tweeple. My daughter was savouring the sights, oblivious to the three of us.

I emptied my glass and waited.

None of them answered my question. I didn't repeat it.

★

On our way back to Kathmandu, I was feeling foul. It had been an utterly useless trip. My daughter looked a little sick on the ride and changed her seat twice.

'What's the matter, Ishita? Are you feeling ill?'

'That smell! What is it?' She wrinkled her nose and turned her head from left to right.

I smelt it then. It lurked in the air somehow, the distinctive smell of marijuana. 'Ganja,' said Subry.

I don't know if she understood. I hoped my daughter would never be trapped by the allure of ganja, strong that it was in its own, intoxicating way. Strong enough to ruin the lives of so many Nepalese men and women. Probably strong enough to propel Sobhraj, my patient-to-be, towards his numb manhunt.

'Go for it, doctor saab,' announced Comrade suddenly, with a smile. 'Say yes to the surgery.'

'Yes, Dai,' Subry nodded too, after what seemed like a pre-planned pause.

★

Until now, I knew Sobhraj only as a serial killer—the 'Serpentine' who was held in seclusion in Golghar, the high-security zone in the Kathmandu Central Jail. He was serving life imprisonment for the murder of a hippie girl. He was a murderer, a convict, and that was all I knew. It had been enough until now; I have never been particularly interested in crime stories. But with Charles about to be my patient, it wasn't enough anymore.

I had an irrepressible urge to know more about him. I started reading articles that had been written about him and his terrible deeds. I watched documentaries made on his life. One thing led to another, and I found I could not stop. I even read a book titled, *The Life and Crimes of Charles Sobhraj* by Richard Neville and Julie Clarke—a rather long and boring book I couldn't believe I finished in record time. I also ordered Thomas Thompson's, *Serpentine*.

3

A CONVERSATION WITH THE LAWYER-IN-LAW

I don't know how people make choices. I am regularly agonized by painful choices. 'Red or white?' my wife asked me on one of our recent shopping trips, pointing to two different shades of a vacuum cleaner and a microwave oven. I broke into a sweat. The ability to answer correctly in these situations is one of the essential secrets to a happy marriage. But it is almost impossible to get these choices right; choosing among colours hasn't been a strong point among most men I know. But what about treating a patient? As a doctor, it should be the one choice that should never frighten or confuse me.

Except, it did.

A part of me wanted to take up Sobhraj's case. But another nagging part steadily refused to do so. Both lingered inside me, tearing me apart.

Doctors are said to be bound by the Hippocratic oath that prohibits them from refusing medical treatment to anyone, on any basis. Being the best student of my batch in medical school, I had enjoyed the rare luxury of standing next to the dean and leading the oath-taking ceremony. But neither the original text in Latin nor its Ukrainian translation at the L'viv Medical Institute had anything about not being allowed to refuse treatment. The fourth point of the Code of Conduct of the Nepal Medical Council did have something to that effect, but I found it incomplete:

> I will not allow consideration of age, sex, religion, nationality, ethnicity, politics, or social standing to intervene between my duty and my patient.

So? I wasn't! He wasn't my patient at all, and government hospitals have a rule against the swapping of doctors without mutual consent. I could just tell Charles Sobhraj that I was following the norms of the medical practice.

I had regular discussions with Comrade, Subry and Anil. They had shed some of their initial reluctance to discuss the matter and wanted to help me tide through my indecision. Poonam, however, was very decisive.

'No. You will not do it. Just tell them so outright.'

While I understood her sentiments, I could not share them fully. One night, I heard her talking on the phone with her father. 'Why is this happening to me?' she said. 'Why is that sick man a part of my life in two different countries, involved with the only two men I love? Is destiny giving me an ominous sign?'

I was sitting on the balcony, sipping tea and brooding over my wife's worries, when Madan, Charles's doctor-in-charge at the Central Jail, called.

'Raamesh, please take over the case of Sobhraj.' No small talk, no background. Here was a senior doctor issuing an order to me, all under the guise of 'please'. I was glad I was finally speaking to a doctor in the know-how of things, someone well-versed with Charles's case. Surely, he could tell me why it was so important that I perform the surgery, even when Navin—the designated surgeon—was fully capable.

'Why must it be me?'

'His plea created a huge drama. That's why we want you to operate.' He paused. I got the feeling that if it hadn't been for the plea and the international media coverage that followed, Charles would have probably been operated upon while I was in Khaptad.

'Dai, I don't understand. He is imprisoned for life, isn't he?'

'Yes.'

'Is there any harm to you, Nepal, or even the mankind if he dies?'

'No.'

'Will you get a promotion if he gets cured?'

'No.'

'Will you face any inquiry if he dies during or after the surgery?'

'No.'

'But he is still important for us?'

'Yes.'

'Then why am I being involved?' I was getting tired of his monosyllabic yes or no answers.

He spoke after a moment or two. 'I am pretty sure Charles Sobhraj will pass his last days in the Golghar. But we cannot afford his death during heart surgery.'

'Why not?'

'Don't be naïve. It would lead to so much international defamation you cannot even imagine!'

'So, you'd rather put my reputation and entire career at risk than risk the life of a convict slated to die one day in jail?'

'You are free to think that way, bhai. Anyway, you are not well known, are you?'

I abruptly disconnected the call. I didn't like the tone that doctor took with me—I don't have false notions of being a world-famous doctor, but I was certainly not inferior to the murderer.

Madan's phone call ruined the rest of the evening for me. I tried to seek some consolation from the India-Pakistan cricket match for the ICC Champion trophy. But it did me no good. I kept waiting for Dhoni to bat, to inch towards 10,000 ODI runs, but his turn never came.

The only good thing that happened that day was that NCell had to cough up 13,600 million rupees as capital gain tax. In a country undergoing political transition, every business house is in a hurry to mint money. The activist in me rejoiced in NCell's loss. I think I also felt proud of my contribution. So much for being an inconsequential doctor!

*

In the hospital the next day, I updated Navin on the proceedings in the Sobhraj case. He was already aware of Charles's refusal. In the wake of the plea and the media attention it garnered, and the growing pressure from the Central Jail and Shakuntala, Navin had no option but to step back.

'Thanks for the courtesy,' he responded flatly.

A bit disconcerted, I headed towards my outpatient clinic. I saw Yakub in the lobby again. With him was a little blue-eyed boy with a cross around his neck. Yakub's organization of religious conversion sure seemed to be flourishing.

'You seem to be making good progress,' I nodded at him before entering my room. He chuckled. The boy looked confused.

Charles was seated inside, accompanied by five cops again. I was getting used to the sight of a convict, policemen and handcuffs inside my clinic. Who was I kidding, of course I was not! I was taken aback each time; it renewed my indecision and increased my fears.

Charles sat there, looking important, exuding the air of a man of lofty stature. I had an enormous urge to show him that he wasn't the most important patient in our hospital.

A young girl, about 24, entered the room. Dr Nivesh, one of my colleagues, also walked in.

'What's your queue number?' I enquired.

'Doctor saab, it is three.'

'Okay,' I said, looking at her lab report, 'What is your problem, Pramila?'

'Dai, she is a victim of domestic violence,' Dr Nivesh replied instead. Pramila had come to the hospital about a fortnight ago, a young woman with two beautiful daughters. She had two metallic valves in her heart and had been advised not to get pregnant again. During her previous pregnancies, she had suffered terribly. After surgery, she was on Warfarin, a blood-thining drug which could cause foetal anomalies as well as serious complications during pregnancy, and may even lead to death. Heart complications never bode well for a bodily challenge as intense as pregnancy. Her husband worked in Dubai—a scenario becoming increasingly common in Nepal due to corruption, political insurgency, and depressingly poor local employment.

'Do your in-laws beat you? Why?' I could guess the answer, but I wanted to hear her say it. Sometimes, voicing your most profound troubles helps you realize strange things, things you are oblivious to even though they are staring at you.

'Saas and sasur want a grandson from me. Otherwise...' Her voice trailed off.

I looked at her young, battered face, some of the bruises hardly concealed by her cheap foundation. Her in-laws, Nivesh told me, had recently erected a four-roomed, cemented house. During their son's next vacation, they desperately wanted a grandson to continue their heritage. Daughters, of course, make 'terrible' heirs.

'Whenever your husband comes home on leave, bring him here. We will counsel him.' I asked Nivesh to check her vital statistics. I wished I could do more, but I couldn't.

Charles was sitting quietly during my meeting with Pramila. He now shifted in his seat. I gestured to him to come over; there was no way I could avoid this confrontation forever.

Very slowly, Charles came near my desk and sat down on the patient's stool. I looked up at him, now at close quarters. His face was puffy, his skin slightly pale. I noticed he was breathing with difficulty and decided to check his pulse.

I touched him.

His hands were cold and clammy. I felt like I was touching a snake. The cover of *Serpentine*—the book I had ordered online and received that morning—flashed in front of my eyes. Was it this coolness that earned him his nickname? Or was he indeed a cold-blooded, venomous snake?

Since my childhood, I have hated poisonous snakes with a vengeance. I loathe the idea of killing anyone with venom, often without any motive other than how they happened to be in your path. Once, I had jumped from one window-grill to the other—an acrobatic feat if there ever was one—to kill a cobra outside my home in Bhadrapur. I have rarely missed an opportunity to kill a snake, not even the Harahara or the grass snake found abundantly in the Nepalese Tarai.

'You do know it is against our religious beliefs to kill a Harahara, don't you?' A classmate asked me once, his voice accusatory. But I didn't reply; it was a beautiful summer day, and I was busy aiming a stick at the head of a serpent. There was sure to be one on the two-mile walk to my school.

When I lived in Ukraine, I met a man called Parkar who hailed from Mumbai, India, and we swiftly became friends. Parkar was fond of conducting bizarre experiments that most people would have dismissed without a second thought. One day, on his way back to medical school from summer vacations, he bought a supposedly non-poisonous rattlesnake from Danilovsky, an Azerbaijani market in Moscow. He fondly named the snake Bublee. I will never forget the first time I touched Bublee. Even though I had killed at least ten snakes by then, I had never touched one directly. I felt the cold skin and shivered; I marvelled at the softness of the serpent eggs. Even in the warm September afternoons, I would pose for photographs with Bublee around my neck. My next-door neighbours would often wake up to rattling sounds at midnight. Surprisingly though, most of them accepted Bublee's cohabitation with us.

It happened one afternoon when we had gone for our classes. I don't know who did it. All we saw, right outside the window of my room, was a dead snake with its head sandwiched between two boulders. A pool of blood had formed near the boulders, congealing rapidly in the late evening breeze. Bublee and I never posed for photographs again.

That day in the clinic, the feel of Charles's hands brought back vivid memories of Bublee. I wanted to go and splash my face with water.

'Show me your legs,' I leaned forward to inspect Charles's feet which were swollen from severe oedema. He was wearing a pair of cheap China-produced shoes—shoes that were in as bad a shape as their owner. He had slipped them on like sandals for the swelling had made it impossible to wear them properly. Charles was a millionaire, or so the newspapers claimed. But I couldn't picture this feeble, ailing man with torn and colourless shoes as someone who owned a private television, accessed the Internet, and partied every night.

I finished his physical examination and then examined his medical records.

The Central Jail Clinic had referred Charles to our National Heart Centre when he complained of shortness of breath. That was on the 10 November 2016. Investigations revealed that he had congestive heart failure due to severely leaking mitral and tricuspid valves—the valves between the two chambers on the left and right sides of the heart. That leakage had eventually led to heart failure and had also elevated the pressure on the blood vessels going to his lungs. He was put on diuretics to help his body produce more urine and offload the excess water.

But his condition did not improve. On 24 February 2017, he was referred to our department for possible surgical management of his leaking valves. Dr Navin had promptly recommended surgery. I remembered that visit. Charles's echocardiography results had come in, showing further dilatation of the left ventricle, the main chamber that pumps blood to the body. The left atrium had already been more than six centimetres in diameter. Navin had advised immediate surgery when I, for some reason still unknown to me, had been tempted to do something peculiar.

'Can I take your picture?'

'Yes!'

And bingo! The serpentine had gotten captured in my frame. Navin had looked askance at me before going on with the consultation. 'We will need to discuss the best option—valve repair or replacement. In the meantime, we will manage your condition medically. It will be best to perform the surgery as soon as possible.'

But Charles had other plans. He had issued a pledge to the Supreme Court, requesting to be granted early release to go to France for the heart surgery. Nepal, he felt, was not capable of succeeding at the complicated surgery involving considerable risk. The news spread like wildfire. Twisted tales and social media posts by celebrities—yes, Randeep Hooda, included—circulated. But the Nepalese government paid no heed.

On 22 May 2017, Charles had been admitted for surgery. The technician had performed a coronary angiogram to look for any narrowed blood vessels going to his heart, a routine procedure for any patient above the age of 45 years. Everything had been set for the surgery.

Except for Charles. He had refused point-blank.

It was around this time that Gyanmani Mama had decided to call a certain man on a leisure trip to Khaptad and had issued him a request that he was never to forget.

'Can I come to you?'

'We will wait.'

★

The lawyer-in-law was staring at me intently. Charles was looking at me too, though his expression was unreadable.

'Okay,' I said. 'I will take up your case.'

Several faces around me broke into a smile. Some of the policemen were smiling too, probably disgusted with these routine trips to the hospital. *He is only a heart patient,* I told myself firmly. *Just a heart patient who needs my help, not a serial killer.* I vowed to myself to quit my obsession with Charles's life and deeds, and treat him like I did my other patients.

'Please get admitted on Friday. You'll have to arrange a targeted blood donor for the surgery,' I told them quickly, without any hint of emotion.

'Thank you, Bhanja. Anything else?'

'Nothing. I'd appreciate it if you wouldn't share anything with the media.'

I was once bitten, twice shy. Some years ago, Mr Girija Prasad Koirala, the prime minister of Nepal at the time, had been admitted to our hospital. He had suffered from shortness of breath. One afternoon, a press reporter had managed to sneak into his cabin, unnoticed by the nurse on duty. It had been all over the papers. 'Who the hell are you to allow reporters in his cabin?' our hospital director had fumed at all of us, angrily crumpling the newspaper with its picture of the sleeping prime minister. 'I'm the only one to break such news to the media!'

I had no desire to repeat anything like that. And this time, it was Charles Sobhraj. In his own right, he was perhaps the most well-known, albeit infamous, person in Nepal.

'Just don't share anything with the media,' I repeated.

4

ADMISSION

On Thursday night, I could not sleep. I sat watching an ongoing cricket match, cheering MS Dhoni as he scored 63 runs in 52 balls. I somehow couldn't accept Mahi as one of the men in blue, a member instead of the captain. But oh well, at least he was inching closer to the milestone I had hoped for him.

When I tried to sleep, forcing my eyes to remain shut, the innocent, pleading face of Mr Chaudhary loomed in front of my eyes. He was seeking justice for his daughter who had died in that fateful road accident I had recently witnessed. 'I want to see the driver behind bars for not following the rules and killing an innocent, law-abiding pedestrian. My daughter was at the zebra crossing; she was a teacher who taught kids to follow traffic rules! And she is no more!' His voice trembled in my frenzied dreams as it did on national television when he broke down at the sight of his young daughter's dead body.

Mr Chaudhary had been fighting for days, but most people knew he would lose the case. Public transport unions were strong enough to bail out the driver. He would lose, just like thousands of others, sinking deeper into sorrow due to the lawlessness in this country.

There were young people, with their entire lives in front of them, killed by the careless. And here I was, about to cure another cold-blooded killer the next day, to prolong his life imprisonment. This killer didn't even have the excuse of being 'careless'.

There was another reason I couldn't sleep that night. Mr Sher Bahadur Deuba, the leader of the Nepali Congress, had been elected the prime minister. And instantly, my nine-month-old tenure as adviser to the health minister had come to an end. At the time, Nepal had almost 50 different parties in the constitutional assembly, and every few months a new coalition was formed to overthrow the previous government. This new chief was renowned for being a coalition expert, i.e., an expert in buying the loyalty of his coalition partners by doling out cabinet posts. There would most likely be a minister for avian creatures and mammals, perhaps further divided into domestic and wild.

★

'Sobhraj is getting admitted today,' I said to Jyotindra, my hospital director, early the next morning.

Admitting a convict to the hospital, especially a notorious man like Sobhraj, involved a fair amount of red tape. There would have to be an official letter from the government, stating that all the medical expenses would be covered by the state. There was security to be considered, the names of the visitors who would be allowed, and the official statement to be issued to the media. The good thing was, all this cumbersome paperwork was the sole responsibility of our legal and accounts department, not the doctors.

'Dr Raamesh, we must have a proper meeting with Ram and the other guys. We cannot afford to make any lapses in security or have the media poking their noses and circulating half-baked stories,' Jyotindra picked up his desk-phone and immediately called Ram, the security-in-charge of our hospital.

It was half past nine in the morning. We were expecting the jail van by eleven.

'Should we keep him in a private cabin?' Ram asked. 'That will be the safest. No one can walk in without a thorough check and prior permission.'

'The government pays only for general beds. Will he pay the surplus himself?' said Upreti, our accountant.

'Forget about the payment! He must not escape. That is our prime concern.' Jyotindra didn't want to risk another media goof-up after what had happened with the prime minister. Even worse was the incident with Jameel Bhati, a Pakistani criminal caught on charges of hoarding fake Indian currency. He was serving his jail term when he suffered a hypertension scare. During his treatment in our hospital, he coined a brilliant plan. In a country where the government was incapable of taking action even against cases of open, publicly-declared bribery, how hard was it for a small-time convict to bribe his way out of the hospital? One fine morning, Jameel walked out of the hospital. Just like that in broad daylight. He was right as rain, wearing his hospital clothes. Apparently, he was unnoticed by two gunmen, a dozen security guards and the entire hospital administration. In a formal report, our hospital claimed that the CCTV cameras had been non-functional. A mere technical glitch had led to the escape of a convict. It was a matter-of-fact incident, as ordinary as someone disobeying the rule of not walking on the grass in the hospital garden.

Jyotindra was probably thinking about Jameel, and how things were infinitely scarier with Charles. If something went wrong, there was no predicting the amount of infamy our hospital would get. 'Another escape from Gangalal, irresponsible director to blame', the papers would say. There could even be legal proceedings—as good as death for the reputation of a hospital. I, however, was worried about other things.

I was, quite self-absorbedly, worried about myself.

Some time ago, there had been a massive ruckus in the Central Jail. An Indian man called Manjeet, allegedly a RAW agent, had been coming down to meet Charles almost regularly. Little known to the jail authorities, he was no RAW agent, but was actually helping Charles hatch his plan of escaping. One fine day, during one of these innocent meetings, Manjeet fired a few shots. Five of them, to be precise. They pierced through the heart of Yunus Ansari, a Pakistani agent serving a jail term. It happened right under the nose of the so-called jail-grade security personnel. If Sobhraj and his allies could pull off such stunts in jail, what was to stop him from bringing an AK-47 or a handmade pistol to the hospital? What if he shot the hospital staff to escape? What if he shot me?

'I can take an elephant through the customs check at Nepal airport,' he had famously questioned the security of Tribhuvan International Airport.

What would stop this man from passing through our feeble, failed-in-the-past hospital security?

✳

He came to my outpatient clinic first, for preliminary scans. I glanced at the policemen accompanying him, peering slyly through my spectacles, and wondered what weapons they possessed. Charles looked frail and sick, seemingly having aged several years in a few weeks. If it had been anyone else, even the prospect of 'escape' would have been ludicrous. But this was Charles Sobhraj.

A few hours earlier, we had completed our preparations for his stay. It was a deluxe cabin, charged at 3,000 rupees a day. We decided to keep his whereabouts a secret—no patient's name on the whiteboard, simply to trick the media. Five gunmen had been designated to guard him continuously. Ram had also requested to keep Sobhraj handcuffed throughout his time in the hospital.

'Do I have to pay?' Charles raised his eyebrows.

'Forget about the pay. Instead, pee.' His creatinine levels, a marker of kidney function, were unnaturally high and constantly rising. A creatinine reading of 211 micrograms per litre was not good news for a patient about to undergo heart surgery. I administered some diuretics and also added a dopamine infusion to his medicine chart. The dopamine, a catecholamine, would help boost his heart's pumping capacity and assist it in delivering more blood to the kidneys.

I am a heart surgeon. I had taken on many challenging cases in the past—cases that demanded swift decisions. 'A surgeon's hands must never shake; his mind must never double guess itself,' one of my professors in medical school would always say. And yet, that day, decisions didn't come easily to me. I knew the slightest error in judgement could set me up for a public trial. In a feudal society, a teenager could be beaten to death for the crime of—or merely the suspicion of—pickpocketing. A girl could be beaten, fed human excreta, and tied to a tree for supposedly being a witch. When the public meted out justice, everyone was the police, the law, the judiciary—all at once. If something happened to Charles, I knew my fate was sealed for me. I would be called Doctor Death until I breathed my last. Success was my only hope of escaping that fate.

I spoke to Charles, 'Whenever you go to the toilet, measure the amount of urine and inform the nurse. Don't forget. I need to know that the drugs are working as they should.'

Charles turned out to be a model patient. By Sunday morning, his urine volume had reached seven litres. The swelling in his leg had gone down considerably, and his breathing had also eased a little. The creatinine levels were down to 180 micrograms per litre. If nothing else, it was a welcome sign that his kidneys could function well, if only the heart would allow it. It made me feel a little better to note that the catecholamine was working; it had managed to power up his heart's contractions, leading to better blood flow to his vital organs, especially his kidneys.

'I feel better, doctor.' Charles gave me a small, watery smile on Sunday afternoon while nibbling at a lychee. Earlier that day, a representative from the French embassy had turned up with a basket of lychees and mangoes. I couldn't imagine why the embassy held him in such high regard, calling every day to inquire about his well-being, sending people with baskets of fruit. If only they gave half of this consideration to our campaign to free the pavement for pedestrians!

By Monday morning, Sobhraj's creatinine levels were down to 155—only a little higher than the average mark. Another significant decision now faced me—the specific type of surgery to perform on his heart valves. I was desperate to conduct a successful operation, to see Charles emerge alive and healthy.

There was no scope for error, human or otherwise.

'When do you plan to operate?' On the day of admission, Shakuntala Didi asked me. 'I am arranging for the blood donors as you asked.'

'Sometime next week,' I said vaguely. Mondays and Thursdays were my operation days, but I had yet to accept the finality of it all.

*

That day in the hospital, the doctor-in-charge of the Central Jail called me again. 'How is Charles doing?' The French embassy called too—'Does Charles need anything?' No one asked me about the type of surgery I was planning. All they cared for was Charles and his recovery, whether that took a valve repair, replacement, or a full-blown miracle.

Meanwhile, my colleagues too did not share my anxiety. People around me worked normally, chatting about Mr Matthias Meyer, the German Ambassador in Nepal. He had captured the public attention—mine too—on the day Charles had been admitted to the hospital. Mr Meyer's tenure was soon to be up, and he had announced a plan to return to Germany via land—a distance of more than 10,000 kilometres. The media didn't miss an opportunity to spice up the news. Even though Meyer's decision emanated from his fear of air travel, here's what the headlines said: 'Aviophobic ambassador plans to traverse the hippie trail, is to travel a distance of more than 10,000 kilometres'. Under the headline was a photograph of the man standing next to a white SUV—a Mitsubishi Pajero. The sky-blue number plate read: '18 CD 4'.

5

A GEM DEALER ON
THE HIPPIE TRAIL

I sit beside the dark, beneath the mire,
Cold grey dusty day,
The morning lake drinks up the sky.
Katmandu, I'll soon be seeing you,
And your strange bewildering time will hold me down.
Pass me my hat and coat, lock up the cabin,
Slow night treat me right, until I go.
Be nice to know, Katmandu I'll soon be touching you,
And your strange bewildering time will hold me down.
Chop me some broken wood, we'll start a fire
White warm, light the dawn,
And help me see Old Satan's tree.
Katmandu, I'll soon be touching you,
And your strange bewildering time will keep me home.

—'Katmandu', by Cat Stevens

There was a time in my life when I was enthusiastic about driving. My mind sometimes, even today, goes back to when Thamel was tranquil and not the hangout place it has now become. The Ganges flowed lazily by. The pungent aroma of ganja lingered at the Benares Ghats. In those days, far-flung places like Tehran and Kabul were still accessible by road.

A number plate flashed in front of my eyes—EHE 839. An orange Volkswagen microbus. There were four young Dutchmen in the microbus, heading east from Amsterdam. These twenty-something men had bought the microbus for a dream tour—the journey they had been saving up for years, the journey that would salvage their soul.

They were generous men, happy, careless, almost reckless. They were ready to add to their group, add to the merriment in their hearts.

A hitchhiker signalled to them, gesturing with his thumb. 'Hi, I am Charles,' said the man, his eyes hidden behind dark sunglasses. 'Are you driving the upper route?'

'Yes, I am Mike,' called out one of the men with a smile. 'For Katmandu.'

'I'm thinking of Benares,' said Lilly, the Dutchman with unkempt hair.

The 'Pudding Shop' in Istanbul, the famous hippie hangout, was the final check-post for their dream journey.

'Don't be over-smart in Istanbul,' said Lilly to his bus-mates. Marijuana and hashish were not easy to come by in Turkey and Iran, and anyone caught with drugs was sure to be jailed for at least a few nights.

They didn't have to wait too long. At Islam-Qala, the Afghan border, the policeman was selling hash. What could be safer? But the Dutchmen and the new hitchhiker resisted the temptation.

The BIT Guide, their hippie guidebook, warned against it. This was a photocopied, stapled treasury of useful information for the road, compiled by frequent travellers and regularly updated with dangerous pitfalls to guard against. No, they would wait to acquire hashish from Herat, only a few kilometres from the border.

Armed with hashish from Herat and cheap shirts from Kandahar, they looked for a place to park the bus. At the Chicken Street of Kabul, they were joined by others—people they had perhaps never met before, but who became friends in a blink. They sat by a big campfire, made by Sigi, the owner of a German restaurant in the area. The fire and the merriment transformed the chilly winter night to a warm, crackling one. Mike strummed 'Katmandu' on his guitar—the Cat Stevens song that resonated with everyone in the group.

> *I sit beside the dark, beneath the mire,*
> *Cold grey dusty day,*
> *The morning lake drinks up the sky.*
> *Katmandu, I'll soon be seeing you.*

Afghanistan had a lot to offer to the men. 'The people here are far friendlier than the ones in Morocco,' said Mike. It was a consensus that almost every hippie with North African experience arrived at in those days. While passing through the Khyber Pass, Mike sat by the rocks at Band-e-Amir and stared at the blue water of the six interconnected lakes. The other men weren't interested in sightseeing; Pakistan held little fascination for them. Some of them disembarked and hurried to Lahore. They would then go to the Wagah border and enter India.

About five men were left in the microbus. 'Two more nights,' Mike said to Charles, passing him a joint. In two more nights, they would cross the Sunauli border to reach Nepal.

Three months went by.

✴

'We have to fix a press meet. Let's organize it today?' said Dev saab, the renowned Indian actor, to his assistant. He was breakfasting at Soaltee, a five-star hotel in Kathmandu.

Dev saab was not in a good mood. He was in Nepal to shoot his new movie, *Hare Rama Hare Krishna*. The previous night, he had shot an important scene of what would turn out to be a famous song, 'Dum Maro Dum', in Kashtamandap. Somehow, the whole thing had been distorted and painted in poor light by *The Rising Nepal*, a government-owned newspaper with a sizable readership in the country. The report had chastised him for ruining the image of Nepal by shooting a movie about drug addiction in one of the country's most sacred, culturally significant spots. Dev saab had an excellent rapport with King Mahendra, the then Nepalese ruler, and had even been invited to stay with him at Pokhara. It was there that Dev saab eventually completed the first draft of *Hare Rama Hare Krishna*, his cult movie about Jasbir, an Indian girl living with a band of hippies in Kathmandu.

'Okay. I will call everyone at once, including reporters from that Rising Nipple,' the assistant chuckled, trying to cheer up his boss.

Meanwhile, in the neighbouring room, a gemstone dealer from France was befriending a hippie girl. 'This is a ruby stone from Rangoon,' said Mr Alain Gauthier. 'See how it shines?'

And at the same time, amidst the thick smoke of hashish, Mike would be playing Jimi Hendrix at the foothill of Monkey Temple with a volunteered chorus from hundreds of hippies.

Well, I'm standing here freezing, inside your golden garden,
Got my ladder leaned up against your wall.
Tonight's the night we planned to run away together,
Come on Dolly Mae, there's no time to stall.
But now you're telling me that ah...
I think we better wait till tomorrow.

★

Kathmandu was one of the three final destinations of the Hippie Trail, along with Goa and Benares. The hotel industry, however, hadn't grown in proportion with the burgeoning tourism. The microbus went from one hotel to another, but the men could not find a place to stay. Eventually, they settled for a small, rather decrepit house in Maruhiti, the 'Pig Gali'. There were several houses in this area—jhonchhe or houses in a row—and it became the new hangout for them. It went into *The BIT Guide* as the 'Freak Street'.

Within a year, the mud houses with the low ceiling had transformed into hotels, restaurants and second-hand bookstores. The number of guests kept on increasing. Seeing that many guests were from the West, taller than the average Nepalese, the shop owners started putting up 'Mind your head' signs above their doors.

The men would go from Maruhiti to Hanuman Dhoka, the Monkey Temple to the Kathmandu Durbar Square. They would sit chatting with Mr Ram Prasad Manandhar, the owner of the Snowman Cake-Pie Shop. He would tell them about The Beatles—perhaps the best-known musical band in the world—and how they were rumoured to have stayed at the Kathmandu Guest House. Bob Dylan too, it was said, had visited the shop.

The men would sit in a dark room in candlelight, talking about the bygone times as well as the times to come. When the wax melted, they would picture a pristine waterfall. At nightfall, they would go to Swayambhunath—a sacred Buddhist Stupa—and smoke the joints freely available there. There would often be a party in one of the houses at the foothills; both hashish and music flowed freely.

There was another place the group frequented—the Hotel Eden and Restaurant. To them, the menu was salvation personified:

Hashish Milk Coffee	₹1.25
Hashish Black Coffee	₹1.00
Hashish Hot Chocolate	₹2.00
Ganja Milk Coffee	₹1.00
Ganja Milk Tea	₹ 0.75
Hashish Lemon Squash	₹1.00
Hashish Lassi	₹2.25
Hashish Toasted Cheese	₹2.50
Hashish Cake	₹1.50
Hashish Chocolate	₹1.50

At a time when one American dollar could buy ten Nepalese rupees, a single rupee was enough to buy a hearty, intoxicating meal. Many of these restaurants offered free stay, or lodging, in return for a mere fifty paisa—in the attic.

Kathmandu was an exciting place at that time. The most scandalous gossip was that Dev Anand had been banned from walking on the streets of Kathmandu, especially when he was dressed in a black suit. Girls, it seemed, were at the risk of jumping out of windows to embrace him. The men, however, were free. When the haze of hashish cleared briefly, they volunteered at the local restaurants. The chefs would share their cooking mastery with the vital ingredient—hashish—and showcase recipes of all sorts, from cakes and pies to toast. Sometimes, the men ran an 'Aden Hashish Centre' and gave away free marijuana and hashish to the broke. It was worth it, really, for the recipients would thank them generously and proceed to savour the treat while ogling at the wooden statues of the Hippie Temple. Much like the sensuous lovemaking postures in Vātsyāyana's *Kamasutra*, this pagoda-style, three-roofed Vishnu temple offered physical release to all who ogled. The love-seeking hippies would leer, inhale and giggle, their faces rapt with almost unearthly delight.

★

'Do you know I had a hot water bath today? It felt like heaven!' Connie was bragging to her new companions in the dining hall of the Oriental Hotel, a popular hitchhiker's den.

'Really? Where?'

'In Hotel Soaltee. Have you seen the big pool they have? If it wasn't so cold, I would have dived into it.'

'So did you?' Laurent, her roommate, put away his chillum. He liked the sound of this pool.

'No. I happened to meet a gem dealer there—a man called Alain. A fascinating guy and so helpful too! He had hot water in the bathroom.'

'You actually bathed in his room?' Laurent enquired, wide-eyed.

'Why are you getting so riled? Every man doesn't see a woman and immediately think of going under her skirt! Alain is not like that.'

Laurent didn't say anything. Connie and their other

companions in the dining hall were in the Christmas mood. Jokes were circulated, someone even came up with a spate of synonyms for 'going under the skirt'. The thick smoke from the chillum made it difficult to see anything properly.

'I'm going to Nagarkot for Christmas,' declared Connie. 'Alain is going to show me the garnet mines there.'

'If it feels good, do it!' The inspirational hippie chant went around the table, everyone but Laurent joining in. In the hippie circle, the most important philosophy was freedom. You did what made you feel free; if you felt limited by someone or something, you had to let them go. It was freedom they sought in marijuana, hashish and other psychedelic drugs. The drug haze, according to them, was liberating, enlightening, even spiritual.

Laurent wanted to change the topic. 'I need some money for a Christmas cake,' he said. 'How much are you willing to offer for this beauty of a book?' He waved his copy of 1984, George Orwell's path-breaking dystopian novel on politics.

'Two and a half!' announced the shopkeeper of the Snowman Cake-Pie Shop. He often joined their group for meals.

'It's yours.' Laurent stuffed the money in the pocket of his jeans. He wanted to buy a little treat for his American girlfriend, his Connie who seemed to be drifting away from him each day. *Today she is with you; tomorrow she may fall out of love. Does she even love you?* He wondered what this Alain guy was like, and why Connie seemed so smitten by him. He took a puff from his chillum and tried to calm down. Unfortunately, hashish didn't stop androgens from reigning supreme in the body. His possessiveness for Connie only grew. She was *his* woman, for god's sake! He decided to throw her a surprise party after returning from that day's tour.

Laurent changed into clean—well, cleaner—clothes. A

generous westerner had invited him to visit Bhaktapur. He wanted to say goodbye to Connie before leaving, to give her a hint about the surprise he was planning for her that evening. But she was nowhere to be seen. *Never mind*, smiled Laurent to himself. That evening, they would spend a glorious time together, exactly like they used to when they had first started dating.

Connie, meanwhile, was riding to the garnet mines in Bhaktapur. She was excited about everything she would see there—the glossy minerals that were eventually transformed to beautiful gemstones.

There were no garnet mines in Bhaktapur. There had never been any.

*

The headlines in *The Rising Nepal* changed overnight. The angry story about Dev Anand's *Hare Rama Hare Krishna* and its alleged tainting of Nepalese heritage was forgotten. The movie had become a blockbuster; Zeenat Aman was now everyone's favourite diva. King Mahendra had a heart attack and passed away. Leonid Brezhnev, an influential new leader of the Soviet Empire, was dreaming about a communist Afghanistan, with Iraq and Iran in tow. But all that was stale, uninteresting news compared to the heinous beast lurking on the hippie trail.

The beast had consumed the imagination of the people in Nepal. He was all anyone could think of or talk about.

When I was a child, there was a street magician who used to come and entertain the crowds. This was in Bhadrapur in eastern Nepal, only a few metres from my school. Bishnu Pratap would show us tricks with decks of cards. While his tricks were perfectly competent, it was something else that we found more exciting. Bishnu Pratap would stand there, thumping his chest with great force, and declare, 'I have a son who is 28 years old.'

What a liar! The man looked no older than our father and yet he claimed to have a son in the late twenties. 'You're a liar!' Some of the kids would chant in unison.

Bishnu Pratap would ignore the kids. He would make a paper rocket and put it inside a glass bottle. 'I will make this rocket fly to the moon.' He would then glare at his spectators— about fifty to hundred children and some curious adults. 'If you don't clap when I order, you will be blind by tomorrow morning!'

We would clap obediently. We would clap when he made the queen of spades vanish. We would clap when he brought the queen back. He would crack an adult joke which few of us would understand. But applaud we would. None of us wanted to become blind.

'Here's the final magic for today, the secret behind my youth. Behold the Shilajit!' Out would come a glittery packet of herbal medicine. 'From gastritis to toothache, fever to poor performance in bed, the Shilajit will cure all your ailments!'

We would clap again, wondering how anyone could perform poorly in bed. How much effort did it take to fall asleep? Fatigued with my studies and snake catching, I would usually doze off within seconds. The adults among the spectators, however, would eagerly purchase the medicine. We would wait while the exchange of money went on, waiting for the rocket to fly.

But the rocket never flew.

One cold December morning, in 1975, the mutilated corpse of an American girl was found in a paddy field near the Manahara River, in the outskirts of Kathmandu. A few days later, another body was found at Sanga, near Bhaktapur. The body belonged to a Canadian hippie.

The magician's rocket had never flown, despite the threats of blindness we had suffered every day. But the golden age of the hippie trail had surely flown away. It had been decimated by the terror of an unknown monster.

★

I think I'm goin' to Katmandu, that's really really where I'm going to,
If I ever get out of here, that's what I'm gonna do.
I got no kick against the west coast, Warner Brothers are such good hosts,
I raise my whisky glass, and give 'em a toast,
I'm sure they know it's true.
I got no rap against the southern states, every time I've been there it's been great,
But now I'm leavin' and I can't be late,
And to myself be true.
That's where I'm goin to Katmandu,
Up to the mountains where I'm going to,
If I ever get out of here, that's what I'm gonna do.
I got no quarrel with the Midwest, the folks out there have given me their best.
I lived there all my life I've been their guest,
I sure have loved it too.
I'm tired of lookin' at the TV news, I'm tired of drivin' hard and payin' dues.
I figure, baby, I've got nothing to lose, I'm tired of being blue,
That's why I'm goin to Katmandu, up to the mountains where

I'm going to.
If I ever get out of here, that's what I'm gonna do.
Katmandu, take me baby cause I'm goin' with you.

—'Katmandu', by Bob Seger

The hippies brought a lot to the eastern world—cakes and apple pies, omelettes and the continental cuisine, Bob Marley and The Beatles, second-hand books by Ernest Hemingway and Hermann Hesse, Volkswagen microbuses, Dev Anand's Jasbir.

And also, inadvertently, a beast.

The Satan of the hippie trail.

6

CHARLES SOBHRAJ, THE SERPENTINE

Truth be told, it wasn't only the beast that decimated the hippie culture. The ongoing conflict in the Middle East and the Soviet invasion of Afghanistan also hit it hard. But in 1976, after the Nepalese government banned cannabis, the hippie culture never revived completely. Cat Stevens probably never managed to see 'Katmandu' and experience the freakish life of grass and hash. He converted some years later to Islam and changed his name to Yusuf, an irony if there ever was one. The intensity of his new conversion became evident when he was asked about Ayatollah Khomeini's death fatwa against the author, Salman Rushdie. After Rushdie's book, *The Satanic Verses,* was published, Khomeini, an Islamic religious leader, ordered the killing of the author for blasphemy against the Prophet. Yusuf had only this to say—'He must be killed.'

It is heartbreaking how killing and killers punctuated the hippie trail, which was once the route to freedom and salvation. Once, a news channel asked Charles Sobhraj, 'What makes a man a murderer?'

'Feeling,' Charles said, simply. 'Either they have too much feeling and cannot control themselves, or they have no feeling. It is always one of the two.'

In all fairness, Yusuf's disillusionment with the hippie trail was not unfounded. Charles, the Satan of this trail, wielded strength and notoriety enough to make anyone wince. Years later, this Satan, however, would be busy measuring the amount of his urine in a small, white-tiled hospital toilet. He would pass out now and then, the plastic beaker with his urine slipping from his hands and spilling on the floor.

★

It was the year 1943, bang in the middle of World War II. Vietnam was war-torn, and, much like any other ravaged country, harboured many homeless children. One of these street children was Noi aka Tran Loang Phun. Children grew up quickly on the streets, hunger and the struggle for survival rapidly eating into their innocence. Noi caught the eye of a wealthy Indian man—a textile merchant who ran the Hatchand Bhawani Prasad Gurumukh Shop. Noi and the textile merchant fell in love, got married, and became parents to a baby boy in 1944. They named the child, Hatchand Bhaonani Gurumukh Charles Sobhraj.

But Noi and Hatchand's marriage was doomed from the start. When he visited his home country, his parents forced him to get married to a girl from Pune in India. 'I am sorry,' he claimed when he was back in Vietnam. 'If it's any consolation, it was purely an arranged marriage. It's not like I love her. You can still stay here as my wife.'

Noi and Hatchand separated. She eventually found a new beau—a French army lieutenant called Jacques Russel—and moved with her new partner to the cantonment. Charles remained with his father in Saigon. Noi's firstborn was soon relegated to the status of the neglected child of warring, estranged parents—the child who didn't fit anywhere.

Noi already had two kids with Russel and was pregnant with the third when he was called back to Marseilles in France. Four years passed by before Russel and Noi got the chance to visit Vietnam. Charles wasn't doing well. His days passed by in neglect, his father's family paying him little attention. On an impulse, fuelled by a sudden burst of emotion for her first baby, Noi decided to take her son away to France. She would help him get a normal childhood, or at least, salvage what remained of it.

But things didn't go as planned. Charles was unable to bond with his new family in France. He would frequently lose his temper and lash out at his mother for separating him from his father. Eventually, Charles turned against his father too, for permitting his ex-wife to take him away. He detested the new ways of his life, the new man who was his mother's husband and whom he was supposed to address as 'dad'. He longed for his life back in Saigon.

It was then that this adolescent boy, for no apparent reason, started committing petty crimes. It would be theft one day, violence the other. He was frequently in and out of the juvenile prisons in France. Each time he was apprehended, his mother's heart broke a little. She meted out harsh punishments for all his crimes; she wanted to do everything in her power to raise her son well. He wouldn't live on the street as she had; he would have a respectable life that didn't have anything to do with prisons. But her punishments only angered Charles further. He got worse. Finally, one day, exhausted with their efforts to reform the boy, Noi and Russell gave up. Charles was sent to a hostel in Paris while they moved back to Saigon. He came to visit them a few times, a young boy of sixteen, his mind and face both equally unreadable.

By now, Charles was a hardened criminal. In 1963, he was caught for a charge of burglary and sent to the Poissy prison near Paris. His term in this Parisian prison was perhaps the last chance he had to pause—and reverse—the infernal storm taking over his soul. But he did not take it. Instead, he learnt to manipulate, to use his charming, seductive personality to get people to do his bidding. He managed to convince the jail authorities to bring him books on literature and foreign languages. He also befriended Felix d'Escogne, a prison volunteer and a wealthy Parisian. The two decided to stay together when Charles was on parole.

While in Poissy, Charles got an intimate exposure to the criminal underworld of France. Felix's friendship took him very close to the Parisian high society. This was not the society Charles hailed from, but he fitted right in; his knowledge of literature and foreign languages wonderfully complemented his handsome personality. With feline grace and cunning, he clawed his way into this world, marrying crime and riches. He *had* to belong to this world now, whatever it took. To maintain the standards he wanted to portray to the world, he was in constant need of money. No wonder then that his favourite crimes—robbing tourists and breaking into houses—continued with increasing momentum.

It was during this time that Charles met Chantal Compagnon, a young and wealthy Parisian girl. Chantal was from a conservative French family. If someone had told her that she would fall in love—head over heels at that—with an Indo-Vietnamese man with a police record, she would have giggled. But that's precisely what happened. Chantal found herself unable to resist this new man in her life; he was everything her heart had ever desired. 'Will you marry me?' Charles asked her one beautiful summer afternoon, looking into her eyes with what could only have been love.

'Of course!' she said.

On the day they were supposed to get married, Charles was arrested. He had been caught stealing a car.

However, nothing could deter Chantal. Her love for Charles was unfailing. Within eight months of his release from prison, the two got married. Within a year of their marriage, Chantal was pregnant with Charles's child. The father-to-be thought nothing of faking cheques and robbing tourists; after all, it was only to make his pregnant wife happy.

★

In 1970, Charles and Chantal travelled to Mumbai in India. He started an innovative venture to make money—selling stolen European cars. It paid well—well enough to start gambling but not enough to last. He needed a lot more money to maintain the living standards he'd been used to in Paris. Robbing tourists and stealing jewellery in India didn't amount to much. So, he gambled more often and staked more money. Pretty soon, his poisonous gambling addiction eroded the earnings from the stolen car business. The family was now bigger—Chantal had given birth to little Usha—and life in Mumbai was expensive.

Charles started hunting for another profitable business.

And he found a golden opportunity.

Late one evening in September, he came across a group of hippies. It was a happy gathering—the smoke, laughter and conversations flowed freely. The men and women looked content, free, reckless. They looked like easy prey.

Pretty soon, Charles started laying down plans to befriend the hippies, a lot easier to target than other foreigners. These were young people from the West visiting South Asia—the 'great India'—to bask in its spiritualism and lap up the mystical Hindu culture. To them, India had an undying charm that existed nowhere else in the world, never mind how it had suffered under extended colonization by the Europeans. India may have been half a century behind the levels of industrialization in the west, but it had preserved the gifts of its ancestral roots. If heaven was up above, too elusive to attain in those times of the Great Depression, the mighty Himalayas and the smoke from the marijuana-filled chillum came a close second to paradise.

Observing a massive influx of white backpackers in India, most of them hippies, Charles decided this was the perfect business venture. Robbing the hippies was easier too; sometimes, both the robbery and the disappearance of the robbed went unnoticed. The police department dismissed the few cases that did get reported, labelling them as 'those dratted hippie robberies'.

One day though, everything changed.

India was grappled by communal tensions, frightening in their severity. While the Wagah border between India and Pakistan was still open, the two countries were up in arms against each other over Bangladesh, then East Pakistan. The influx of hippies lessened to almost zilch. Charles was frantic;

he was also furious that political scenarios had interfered with his convenient and quick money-making venture. It was time to go big.

Charles laid down a meticulous plan to conduct an armed robbery in Hotel Ashoka, New Delhi. His eyes were set on a jewellery shop with gleaming gems for display. But luck wasn't with him then—he was caught and imprisoned. The irrepressible con man feigned an attack of acute appendicitis, only a week after being caught. At Willingdon hospital, where he was admitted for treatment, Charles waited for a blackout. Long power blackouts were regular in Delhi at that time—one of the many evils of the ongoing war. During one of these blackouts, Charles managed to drug the guard and escape. It was a short-lived escape, for both Charles and Chantal were caught at the railway station— but the whole episode was highly productive for the deceptive criminal. He now knew for sure—his armamentarium worked! Drugs were more potent than he had imagined, if only he could use them optimally.

After Charles was released from jail, he started his final— and most menacing—venture. Usha had been sent to France. The couple, now without any family ties and not even a hint of scruple left in their souls, departed on a hippie manhunt.

The two moved down the trail like predators, scouting for prey. Hashish lovers were abundant in Chicken Street, Kabul. From their base at the Hotel Intercontinental, they befriended and eventually robbed countless hippies.

In early 1972, Charles was arrested again; he hadn't paid the hotel bills. But for a criminal adept at escaping from high-security prisons, a 'petty' offence like not paying the bills was almost a joke. How could it keep him down? He escaped—with laughable ease—by drugging a guard. Chantal, the woman who had been with him for years, had seen his wicked ways and supported them in full measure, was left alone. Her love for him meant nothing—it was not enough for him to keep her in his thoughts before fleeing. After being let out of Kabul jail, she moved back to France and joined her daughter. Her days of shadowing Charles, the man who had finally robbed her, much like the hippies, were over.

Charles didn't mind. His carefree, luxurious life with women, weed and money was far more important than some woman who, by now, had lost her initial lustre. He travelled easily, moving across borders with fake passports acquired from the hippies. His exceptional knowledge of drugs and languages came in handy.

In 1974, Charles was arrested again—this time in Greece. He had been stealing jewellery. Even though Charles was sent to the toughest prison in the country—Aegina Island—he escaped. Again. A mysterious fire broke out in the van that was taking him to a hospital. It was after this incident that he got the nickname 'Serpentine'—the one who slithers on the grass unnoticed, impossible to catch. The one whose bite is lethal.

'The police may wish to keep me in prison throughout my life. But they can never defeat my will to be free.' Charles was rumoured to avow, as quoted by Richard Neville in his book, *The Life and Crimes of Charles Sobhraj.* 'I can escape at will. I can rob at will. I can live exactly as I want.'

The hippie trail had a new god—equal parts captivating and petrifying.

★

It was the time of Emergency in India. Indira Gandhi, who was then the Indian prime minister, had imposed a state of political deadlock to counter suspected threats to national security. Every day, political leaders and civilians were arrested, the prisons filling up fast. It was turbulent enough to daunt even Charles, especially after he narrowly escaped being arrested on a few occasions. By then, he had developed quite a reputation amongst the police; they distinctly remembered him from the Ashoka Hotel robbery. It wouldn't do to stay in India anymore. He had to move out to safer, greener pastures.

Not that going out of the country was any hassle for him. He had multiple fake passports, all with photographs uncannily resembling him. If they didn't, Charles would merely throw on a disguise. At immigration checkpoints, they would take one look at his handsome, sophisticated demeanour, quickly inspect the passport, and tell him to 'please proceed.' He would stay at his rented apartment in Bangkok and move freely through Asia.

He became known as quite the charmer in Bangkok. The handsome, smooth man with a seemingly generous heart, especially towards young hippies, swiftly became the darling of the murky social circles in Bangkok. His new identity as a gem dealer started attracting more hippies to his den. To keep up with the growing business, he befriended two people who became his partners—the Canadian, Marie-Andrée Leclerc, and the Indian, Ajay Choudhury. It was all very well for a while; the three of them successfully dealt with hippies and minted money. But there soon came a point when the leader of the pack had had enough. He had to get rid of the broken creatures; they knew too much. How could he get rid of them for the well-being of his business? The question did not demand much thought.

The young man of 32 had only one solution.

★

18 October 1975. Pattaya, Thailand. The body of a young white girl in a floral bikini was floating on the shallow water near the shore. She had probably drowned under the influence of drugs; it wasn't all that uncommon in Thailand. Teresa Knowlton, a 24-year-old woman from Seattle, was en route to Kathmandu to learn meditation at one of the Buddhist monasteries. Perhaps she realized that drugs were a faster route to salvation than learning to meditate? It was only a long time later that an autopsy was conducted on her dead body. She hadn't drowned. Someone had strangulated her to death and then tossed her body in the water.

28 November 1975. The road to Pattaya Resort, Thailand. The charred body of a foreigner was found by the roadside. The man turned out to be Vitali Hakim, a Sephardi Jew from Ibiza. The autopsy revealed a horrible truth—Vitali had been attacked, his body mutilated, drenched in a pool of gasoline, and then burnt. He had been alive when set ablaze.

16 December 1975. Pattaya beach, Thailand. The sea was throwing up dead human bodies by the dozen. This time it was a woman again, her lifeless young body floating under the coastal sky. Investigations revealed that it was Charmayne Carrou—Vitali Hakim's French girlfriend—who had come down to investigate her boyfriend's disappearance. She too had been strangulated to death and thrown into the water. Her neck was broken; there had probably been quite a struggle. Or the murderer had simply taken sadistic delight in breaking her neck after ending her life. The Thai media went hysterical; they brought out one story after another about the 'Bikini Killer' who had slaughtered two women in close succession, both of whom had been wearing swimsuits.

18 December 1975. Pattaya, Thailand. Henricus Bintanja

and his fiancée, Cornelia Hemker, were on their dream tour—
the vacation they had been planning for nearly three years.
The Dutch couple happened to meet a gem dealer—a polite,
good-looking man—who showed them a stunning sapphire
ring. The ring gleamed under the sunlight, reflecting all the
colours of the sea. Two days later, however, their bodies were
dark, charred and lifeless. In a secluded place near Pattaya, the
Dutch couple lay dead. The autopsy confirmed what the police
already suspected—they too had been alive when the flames
overpowered them.

But one riddle baffled the police no end. Henricus Bintanja
and his fiancée were flying out of Thailand on 18 December
1975, the same day their dead bodies were discovered. Their
names were found onboard the Kathmandu-bound flight of the
Royal Nepal Airlines.

The deaths did not stop; the killings only became more
gruesome.

23 December 1975. A paddy field near Manahara River,
east of Tribhuvan International Airport, Kathmandu, Nepal.
Passers-by discovered a severely mutilated, charred corpse of
a young westerner. Connie Jo Bronzich from Santa Cruz had
been struggling to breathe when she was burnt alive.

24 December 1975. Sanga, Bhaktapur, Nepal. A burnt body
lay by the roadside, almost disguised by the thick forest. The
young Canadian's body was not discovered until a few days after
his death. By then, Laurent Edmund Carriere had, apparently,
already flown out of the country. The immigration officer at
Tribhuvan International Airport stamped 'Departure' on his
passport while his body lay in the quiet of the jungle, unseen
by everyone but the birds flying overhead.

June 1976. Goa, India. A young French traveller, Jean-Luc

Solomon, was discovered dead in his hotel room. While his death was supposedly from poisoning, his passport and money were missing from his belongings.

5 July 1976. Charles Sobhraj, who had, by then, murdered countless people in cold blood, committed the deadly mistake that is the undoing of any criminal—he became overconfident. He hatched a plan—probably his cruellest yet—to poison and rob dozens of French schoolchildren in Vikram Hotel, India. The plan backfired. Charles was arrested by the Indian police. He was also charged with the murder of Jean-Luc Solomon, passport forgery, theft, and drugging of people. The Indian Court sentenced him to 12 years of imprisonment. After the sentence, Charles was taken to Tihar jail, the toughest prison in India, and put behind bars.

'I didn't kill good people,' Charles said, several years later, in a taped interview with Richard Neville. *Only those he thought deserved it.*

7

THE QUESTION

This was the man now sitting in front of me—the murderer of more than a dozen people, the killer perfectly capable of burning people alive and breaking their necks. What made him do it? Was it only the insatiable greed for money or the inhuman thirst for blood? In his presence, I felt unnerved and fearful. I often found myself tempted to ask. It wouldn't matter how brilliantly, how truthfully he answered, if at all. It wouldn't change anything I felt about him. Nonetheless, I found my curiosity quite impossible to quash.

I have always been intrigued by the power of questioning. As a doctor, it is part of my job to ask the right questions to make the patient comfortable and to get the correct facts. But I will admit, sometimes, I enjoy questioning because I can do it from a position of power. Like the fresh college graduate being interviewed for his first job, the receiver of my questions finds it difficult to breathe. He answers each question after a pause, wiping cold sweat from his forehead.

A few years back, I had applied for a tourist visa to the United States of America. Although I understand that the USA struggles with a fair amount of illegal immigration, I sometimes find myself vexed by the way they treat everyone. As I stood in line, awaiting my turn for questioning, I overheard what happened with a young Nepalese man. It was one of the strangest interviews I have witnessed in my life.

'Why do you want to go to the States?' The man on the other side of the counter enquired.

'I want to export handicrafts from Nepal.'

'And your family?'

'My wife is pregnant.'

'Oh! Then she needs you during her delivery. Sorry!'

That was it; the young Nepalese was rejected entry to the USA. The logic of the man in authority was obviously skewed— he hadn't even asked how far along the wife was. But it was enough to dismiss the case. The Nepalese man kept pleading with him to check his documents until he was dismissed with a peremptory 'Next!'

Yes, I too wanted to question Charles with that kind of authority.

*

On Saturday morning, I sat in my living room reading the newspaper. It was the *Koseli*, a leisure supplement of the *Kantipur*, one of the leading Nepali newspaper. On weekends, the *Koseli* always had an interesting mix of stories. Someone had written about his night-out at Khaptad. In Jhingrana hotel, he had a terrifying experience—he saw the owner fighting loudly with his wife, several colourful cuss words thrown in. 'I know you're planning to elope with the guest! Don't lie to me!' The owner had screamed, his voice rudely piercing the thin walls of the guest room. I chuckled to myself, thanking our stars that we had left Jhingrana when we did. There was news about the German embassy too—the ambassador had left in his white Mitsubishi, 18 CD 4, set to traverse the hippie trail and cover thousands of miles to reach home.

There was also an avalanche of news about Charles Sobhraj. 'Sobhraj admitted to Kathmandu National Heart Centre, surgery is imminent,' declared the headlines. I was not surprised. Even though the entire hospital staff had been instructed to zip their lips about Charles's surgeon-in-charge and course of treatment, who could stop the media from spinning yarns? 'He should have been operated yesterday,' claimed one journalist. From the report, I somehow sensed the source of that incorrect byte— Nihita Biswas, Shakuntala's daughter and Sobhraj's sweetheart.

The next morning, I started my hospital rounds early. 'How many patients?' I asked Ansu who was holding a list of names.

'Six or seven in surgery. There are about 24 patients in the hospital and three new referrals.' I sighed. Performing six open-heart surgeries on three operating tables in a government hospital was a herculean task. But the administration never stopped squeezing in some more, sprinkling the requests with 'please' to the doctors and 'you need to be faster' to the anaesthesiologists and operating nurses.

I checked the list. 'Okay. Put him second.' I inhaled deeply and headed towards his cabin.

All the private cabins in the hospital were on the first floor of the southern wing. A big door opened to a nursing station on the left and a long corridor in front. There were cabins on both sides. And there, on a big whiteboard near the nursing station, it was written in neat lettering:

Deluxe cabin 2. Charles Sobhraj. Severe mitral and tricuspid regurgitations for valve repair or replacement.

I was not pleased. Here were all the details vividly explained for public display. What a relief my name hadn't been put up too! 'Who wrote that?' I asked.

'Sorry, doctor. Someone from the night staff must have done that. She was new here,' said Bidhya, the nurse in-charge, and quickly wiped the board clean.

There were five police officers in the common room, one of them still asleep on a mat on the floor. His uniform was piled up in an armchair. Charles, however, was up. He was sitting in bed, nibbling on lychees again.

'How are you? Did you sleep well?' I asked flatly. It was a standard question. Plus, I needed to know if he was comfortable while lying down.

'Oh, I am better, doctor. Last night, I could sleep with only one pillow.'

That was good; a lot of the excess water in his lungs must have been drained. I approached him to auscultate his lungs.

'Have some lychee.'

I denied instantly. '*Kina lychee matra khayeko? Bhat pani kaye hunchha ni?*' I asked him in Nepali why he regularly consumed lychees and other dry foods instead of the more nourishing rice and lentil soup.

But he looked at me with a vague expression, as if he hadn't understood a word.

I was convinced he knew Nepali. Why was he pretending?

I wondered if it had to do with the cop who was standing near the bed, watching the proceedings. Charles probably forgot all his Nepali in front of police officers. It must have been arduous to pretend like that, all the time, for so many years. But then, this was the master of hoodwinking.

'Did you get all the blood donors ready?'

'Already.'

It must have been a cakewalk for him. He was a convict of high status, and some volunteers were always willing to donate blood to people occupying the limelight. Other than Nihita, a Mr Karki had been crossmatched as a suitable donor. In Nepal, it wasn't easy to get an assured supply of fresh blood at the national blood bank. Cryo-concentrates of blood clotting factors were not available at all. Doctors had to advise targeted donation by volunteers.

Later that day, the stored blood components were brought to the hospital. The donation of fresh blood would be carried out on the day of the surgery.

'Then, you are on for tomorrow.'

Charles stared at me, shocked. Was he afraid of the operation? Did he have a fear of needles? Both scenarios seemed highly unlikely to me.

He spoke to me softly after a moment. 'Doctor, can you postpone the surgery for a few days? Look, my leg swelling has gone down, and I am feeling better. A few more days of rest will do me good.'

I was beside myself with agitation. I couldn't believe he was requesting me to delay the surgery after having pursued me relentlessly—along with his entourage—for an early operation. 'Listen, Charles. This is not negotiable. I cannot keep you here endlessly and perform the surgery on a day that suits you. I had to pull a lot of strings and make adjustments to accommodate you early.'

His expression changed a little. I don't think he had expected me to refuse his demand. I decided to explain things medically to him. 'Here's what I plan to do. Tomorrow, I will try to repair the left valve of your heart. You'll be fine if that works well. But if the valve shows even a small leak, I will have to replace it with prosthetic tissue. Is that okay with you? Or would you rather live with a slight leak in the valve and perhaps undergo another surgery in the future?'

Charles didn't look interested in the gritty details of his heart ailment. 'Do whatever you think is right for me, doctor. I just want to live.'

'Okay, don't worry. And please don't share anything with the journalists here. Keep it to yourself.' I left the room, hurriedly disappearing down the corridor before anyone could stop me for a chat.

*

Subita spoke to me excitedly. She was bursting with the need to say something. 'Sir, do you know he broke into tears when I told him there was a 2 per cent chance of operative mortality? He actually cried!'

I nodded, unsure how to react to that. 'Who signed the consent form as his guardian? His wife?'

'No. He said she cannot as she's not yet legally married to him. An officer from the French embassy signed the form instead.'

Subita and I were discussing the surgeries planned for the next day. She, of course, was most interested in case number 2.

'Sir, why did he kill people?'

That question again. My urge to hear the answer from the

horse's mouth returned in full intensity. 'Feeling,' I told her, quoting Charles. 'Either he had too much feeling and could not control himself, or he had no feeling. It is one of the two.'

The right person to answer her question was eating lychee in a deluxe hospital cabin. I tried to focus on the preparation for the surgery, but Subita's curiosity kept getting the better of her.

'But how could he travel with fake documents? Didn't they look at the photographs?' I wondered briefly if she had experienced a piercing stare or two from an immigration officer while travelling overseas. She sounded miffed.

Nivesh spoke up. 'They often look only at the colour of your passport and the country issuing it. Criminals get by easily; it is only people like you and me who get scrutinized!'

Come to think of it, it *was* unsettling. Charles had travelled all across Asia with fake passports. He was instantly given visas on arrival. And yet, many people I know had experienced cross-questioning as gruelling as a court proceeding, even when they had only been shopping at duty-free shops. Anyone, it seemed, could ask you to produce your green passport and shoot questions, many of them unnecessary and humiliating.

About a decade ago, I was returning from a trip to Dallas. I had been visiting as a medical escort to the International Organization for Migration—an organization facilitating the repatriation of Bhutanese refugees. At Fort Worth, I produced my passport at the ticket counter.

'Oh! You are Nepalese. What are you doing here in Dallas?' A slightly obese white man asked me rather rudely.

'I am on my way back,' I answered casually. I had a valid visa for the USA and was there only to get a boarding pass for the domestic flight to JFK. I didn't feel compelled to tell him the full story.

'Do you have a return ticket from New York to Katmandu?' He persisted. His tone was even sharper than an officer from the Department of Homeland Security.

'Hey, man! Look, you are an employee of Delta. Why don't you do what your job description entails? You're here to check my ticket and give me a boarding pass. That's all! My next destination shouldn't bother you. Let me tell you anyway. I'm going to New York. Then I will go to Los Angeles and meet Arnold. Then I am going to Las Vegas to try my luck at the casinos. Do you have any problem?' I perhaps said more than I had intended to, but by that point in the trip, I was frustrated by the constant suspicion. I couldn't help myself.

He scowled at me and fiddled with his computer. 'So, you are returning tonight by Qatar Airlines.'

'So?'

'You will stay at Doha for five hours, but you don't have a visa for Qatar. Let me see; there's Mongolia, Mozambique, Myanmar, Namibia, Nauru…nope, you Nepalese people are not allowed to get an on-arrival visa in Qatar. Without a pre-issued transit visa, you cannot go to Doha, my man!' He didn't whistle with joy, but I heard the whistling nevertheless.

I seethed with anger. What an irony it was that a man-killing monster had passed through the gates of the airport with no one even checking the photograph carefully, but I was stranded, even with a valid visa, a return ticket, and no criminal record! I wouldn't have been surprised if he had proceeded to ask me about my meals and whether I had paid for the sandwich I carried in my handbag.

'Are you daft? Do you understand that I can easily buy another ticket via New Delhi? I'm even free to buy a jet and fly directly to Kathmandu. Why are you harassing me?'

'Guess what, I visited Katmandu many years ago.' He deigned to smile.

I didn't understand what he meant, but I forced a smile too. Smiling was preferable to the scowling match we had been waging.

'I was a hippie there.'

I exhaled deeply. The author Paulo Coelho was not alone on the hippie trail. Here was another, destined to meet me and torture me at the Fort Worth Airport in Texas. He wasted my time for half an hour, teaching me the immigration law of Qatar. He attacked my low-grade passport; although he wasn't straightforward about it, the suggested inferiority was even more infuriating. The conversation ended only when I threatened to lodge a complaint against him with Delta and the airport authority.

Sometimes, I still feel humiliated by the incident. It seems unpardonable to me that a fair-skinned man instantly becomes a 'saheb', someone who can commit no wrong, even if he is a murderer hunting for his next prey. Criminals roam around like Bengal tigers in the Sundarbans while we have to tread with caution; every step we take is scrutinized with an eagle eye.

Indeed, our powerlessness to question was to blame. We didn't challenge the injustice expended to us; we just accepted it as our fate.

My discussion with Subita and Nivesh that day, unknown to them, encouraged me to go ahead and ask. It would satiate my curiosity. It almost felt like revenge, although I am not sure why.

The question I wanted to ask, however, was not about travel documents and visas.

*

The usual questions I asked my patients pertained to their health and well-being. They were usually answered truthfully too, except for, 'Do you smoke?' But the question I now wanted to ask was much more personal than 'Are you married?' or 'Have you ever experienced a blackout?' By now, I didn't even want to ask him why he had killed all those people.

No, the question that was eating me from within was different.

In 2003, there were nearly 190 countries in the world. Charles Sobhraj was free and living a happy life in France. He was a celebrity, believed to be making a hefty sum of money from interviews and photo sessions. He even had a million-dollar contract with an Indian film-maker who wanted to make his biopic. His jail term in India was over; the Thai police had closed the cases of the murders. Only one country in the world had active cases of murder against him—Nepal. And yet it was Nepal that Charles decided to visit, again. He returned to the country that suspected him of killing foreigners on the hippie trail, of robbing them and fleeing from the spot. He had no apparent reason to return, not unless he was persuaded by the slogan of our tourism department—'Visit Nepal. Once is not enough!'

WHY on earth did he come to Nepal only to find himself behind bars? Was he merely overconfident? Or was there something I was missing, a piece in the jigsaw I had lost altogether?

I had to find the answer.

8

THE SERPENTINE MAKES
ANOTHER ESCAPE

'Come and sit here, saheb,' a police officer at Tihar jail got up from his chair to make space for the man who had just entered his cabin.

Charles Sobhraj smiled a little, nodding at the policeman.

My father-in-law would sometimes regale us with stories of Charles, during his imprisonment at Tihar jail. Poonam's father was a junior-level police official and privy to some information about the convict.

'Papa, he is a criminal. Tell me again why he is treated with so much respect?' I had asked my father-in-law.

'I don't know. Our seniors adore him, and we follow suit.'

'*Naam ho ya badnaam, bas gumnaam na ho.*' Thus went an Indian proverb that perhaps described the special treatment Charles garnered even in jail. Be famous or infamous but not anonymous. Reputation mattered a lot in India, even a bad one!

Charles had been imprisoned with two of his companions. During their trial, both of them attempted suicide in prison. But not Charles. He wasn't giving up that easily.

It was rumoured that Charles concealed precious gems in his body which he used to bribe his captors. It was this bribery that earned him the comforts he enjoyed in prison. If there was something Charles detested, it was mixing with the background, becoming a wallflower. With him, everything had to be striking. He turned his trial into a public spectacle, hiring and firing lawyers whenever he fancied, bringing in his brother—who was on parole—to assist him. He even threatened the Indian government with a hunger strike.

A cold-blooded murderer like him was sure to get the death penalty, or so everyone thought.

All he got was 12 years in prison. 12! His partner Marrie Leclerc was found guilty of drugging the French students. However, she was eventually diagnosed with ovarian cancer and sent back to Canada. She succumbed to death in April 1984.

Meanwhile, Charles lived the good life in Tihar jail. He had more luxury in prison than many can afford at home after years of toil. Many ugly details of his lavish lifestyle as a convict became public in 1980 when the Supreme Court ordered an inquiry into the matter. Subodh Markandeya, a Supreme Court advocate, made a series of visits to Tihar and published a report.

In his report, Subodh shared that Charles Sobhraj had established himself as the 'don' of Tihar. There was a controlling clique arpund Charles, consisting of three bank robbery convicts. The group made merry, violated rules, and misbehaved with the other inmates of the jail. No one dared to oppose them.

There were no restrictions on Charles Sobhraj; he could beat anyone, give interviews as he pleased, and visit any ward at any time. Things seemed well laid out to make his stay as pleasant as possible. Sex and other kinds of entertainment were an integral part of his life in Tihar. There were some other luxuries too—Sobhraj, Jaggi and Kapur had access to television, boys to sodomize, and regular clothes.

The report evidently stated facts. Based on interviews that Charles had given from jail, two books had already emerged in the market—*The Life and Crimes of Charles Sobhraj* and *Serpentine*. The medical officer of the jail had revealed that Sobhraj could often be seen in semi-hidden rooms, making out with a female accomplice. But truthful as it was, Markandeya's report didn't change anything.

Sobhraj continued to be the king of Tihar. In their bid to protect the empire, the gang slept with a revolver in their cell. The gun was never detected; it was smartly passed from cell to cell whenever a search was done. No one dared to confront the lion in his formidable den. Sobhraj behaved as if he owned the place. On occasions, he even shared a cup of tea with the prison superintendent.

One day, a reputed police offer arrived at Tihar; she had the reputation of a national hero. But reportedly, Ms. Kiran Bedi too couldn't do much to change Charles's lifestyle. Instead, she was taken aback by the apparent 'reform' that was palpable in his personality.

A reporter asked her during a press meet, 'How is Sobhraj's behaviour in jail?'

'Oh, Charles has changed! Meditation has helped him a lot. He plans to work with Mother Teresa when he is released. He is completely rehabilitated!' Bedi, the officer-in-charge, replied joyfully. Indeed, how reassuring it was when a jail term reformed you from within!

It is possible that Charles too shared Kiran Bedi's sentiments. 'I never killed good people,' was his constant refrain; his 'cleansing' had a reason. Perhaps he fancied himself to be as humanitarian as Mother Teresa, albeit differently, wiping the world clean of drug-addict hippies and teaching the Western imperialists a well-deserved lesson for colonizing Asia. It was all for a 'good cause'.

*

There was something else that Charles spent time doing in Tihar when he took a break from his lap of luxury—learning about the Indian law.

In 1977, Thailand had issued an arrest warrant for Charles. Since India and Thailand had a treaty on extradition, his trial in Thailand was imminent as soon as he was released from Tihar. It was most likely to be a death sentence since the charges against him in Thailand were unpardonable—the gruesome murder of at least five people. His legal books, which the prison guards were only too happy to provide, taught him an important thing about Thai law. If a suspect was not caught and brought to trial within 20 years of the offence, the charges were automatically dropped. He knew now that there were only two options: one, to face trial—and most likely, death—in Thailand, and two, to avoid extradition at all cost.

It wasn't a difficult choice.

On 16 March 1986, Sobhraj ordered sweets and fruits. His birthday was coming up, and he wanted to treat the prison staff. It was a Sunday, and only a tiny fraction of the staff was on duty. Between 1:00 and 3:00 p.m. that afternoon, Sobhraj threw a party. Everyone enjoyed the sweets and the fruits; the grapes were especially succulent. Within no time, no one but Sobhraj was conscious. Everyone else had passed out under the influence of Larpose—a sedative infused in the food. Charles Sobhraj nonchalantly walked out of Tihar, the toughest prison in India, as if it was the most natural thing in the world.

★

A4, Delhi Police Colony, Kingsway Camp, New Delhi.

Inside a police quarter in New Delhi, a family watched the television with horror. They were all women. Among them was a little girl called Poonam who first looked at one member of her family, and then at another, unable to understand why they looked so harrowed. Sharmaji, the sole male member of the family, was missing. He had gone to his ancestral home in Ghasoli, a small village between Sonipat and Panipat, about a hundred kilometres from Delhi. His mother was seriously ill, and he had been attending to her for the last five days. Sharmaji was one of the patrollers at Tihar—the prison from where Charles had organized a spectacular escape, only a few hours ago.

Some days back, I asked my father-in-law, 'Didn't the media suspect a connection between your leave and his escape?' I didn't particularly want to bring up his memories of the incident, but ever since I had taken up Charles's case, he had become quite interested.

'We didn't have this paparazzi-style media back then. Have you watched *Peepli Live*?' He poured some more whisky in his glass and topped it up with soda. After taking a large sip and biting into a salted cashew nut, he continued, 'Well, the media then wasn't like that, but my department did initiate a probe.

For no fault of mine, I was a suspect for nearly two months. Suspended for no reason!'

'What happened to your colleagues who were on duty at that time?' I sipped from my glass of diluted whisky. It tasted terrible; I would have preferred beer.

'Oh, dozens of them were sacked. Sometimes I am glad Ma was ill at that time. It was a blessing in disguise. If I had been around, I too would have probably been sacked for being an aide to Sobhraj.'

I believed my father-in-law.

*

6 April 1986. Charles was arrested by the Bombay Police. He had been hiding in Goa. It had been only three weeks since his escape. He was taken back to New Delhi and thrown into a maximum-security cell. This time, he was handcuffed and fettered in isolation and was not allowed to mix with other inmates. A 10-year sentence for jailbreak was added to the charges against him. Just like he had calculated.

As the years passed by, the tight security loosened. Sobhraj was allowed to fraternize with others. He started befriending Western journalists who were keen to get bytes on his story. They would visit him in jail, and he would talk openly—and grandly—of his murders. He never admitted to them but maintained that his actions were purely in protest against Western imperialism in Asia.

To Richard Neville, Charles said, 'If I have ever killed or ordered killings, it is purely for reasons of business. It is just a job, much like a general in the army.'

17 February 1997. Twenty years had passed by since he was first jailed for murder. More than twenty years had passed since Thailand had issued an arrest warrant against him. Charles

Sobhraj was released on bail from Tihar; he had managed to deposit the bail amount with the help of an old cellmate. A court hearing was scheduled to decide his fate since his extradition warrant from Thailand had expired and he didn't possess any legal travel and identity documents. During this time, he was kept in custody at a police station.

Eventually, the Indian government decided to deport Sobhraj to France. He had always claimed French nationality, having been born in Vietnam when it was under French rule. The government also withdrew all pending cases against him. They had had enough. Keeping Charles in India any longer was a potential law-and-order landmine that was best kept far away.

But there was another challenge to be overcome. The French government denied India's request to provide travel documents to Charles. It was pure coincidence—and a very fortunate one for Charles—that something miraculous happened just then. Five French fishermen were arrested by Indian naval guards for entering Indian waters illegally. The French government wanted their release. In return, India asked for the travel documents. The bargain, whose ethical and legal undercurrents are debatable, worked.

For the first time, Charles Sobhraj had his identity. He had a travel document in his name. He was not a stateless man anymore, but a French national with an authentic passport. The photograph in the passport was his. On 8 April 1997, 53-year-old Charles Sobhraj was deported to France in an Air France flight. The press crowded into the Charles De Gaulle airport, awaiting the arrival of the criminal celebrity. The man had to be detained at the airport for several hours while the authorities waited for the hordes of press reporters to leave.

✴

Charles settled in the suburbs of Paris to enjoy his retirement—a retirement from crime. He maintained telephonic contact with his lawyer. He also hired an agent and started charging a colossal sum for personal interviews and photographs. An Indian film-maker reportedly signed a deal with Charles— an agreement worth seven million pounds for the permission to make a biopic on his life. Sorab Irani, the managing director of the film production house, called it the story of a 'snake that bites, slides away, sheds its skin, changes colour, and reappears to bite again!' This was a true-blue celebrity snake that loved every moment in the limelight.

It was 1 September 2003. A Boeing landed in the Tribhuvan International Airport of Kathmandu. One of the passengers was called Hatchand Bhaonani Gurumukh Charles Sobhraj. The man strolled around the streets of Kathmandu, visiting casinos and trying his luck. The city was lush green, the jungles thick, young people milling about, enjoying themselves. But Charles was not one to fade into the background; he was not just another face in the crowd. A journalist spotted him and published his picture in *The Himalayan Times*, an English national newspaper in Nepal. Two days later, on 19 September 2003, he was arrested by the Nepalese police from the Casino Royale.

'This is my first visit to Nepal,' he told the press in Kathmandu.

But his crimes had finally caught up with him. On 20 August 2004, the Kathmandu District Court found Charles Sobhraj guilty of the 1975 murder of Connie Jo Bronzich, an American girl. The charges of passport forgery and illegal travel were also upheld. Sobhraj was sentenced to life imprisonment.

It seemed that a substantial portion of the evidence was provided by Herman Knippenberg, a Dutch investigator from Interpol. He had been collecting documentary evidence against Charles Sobhraj for almost 30 years.

9

THE DAY

12 June 2017, Monday.

Everything was set. The stage was prepared. The actors were ready.

'I will finish the bypass case in theatre two,' I instructed Nivesh. 'Meanwhile, you can prepare things in theatre one. We will then switch.'

When I came out of the changing room, wearing my green gown, I saw him in the waiting room. He looked at me nervously. There was none of the slick smiling and manoeuvring. 'I want to live,' he repeated, to no one in particular. That was all I had heard for the last two weeks.

I was stunned to see the tears in his eyes. The fear of death lurked around him, weakening the already frail man. For the last three days, he had been losing large amounts of sodium from his body. He was urinating all the time, getting more and more dehydrated. We had tried to supplement his salt intake with six to eight capsules of table salt. The usual practice is to replace the contents of Vitamin B complex capsules with table salt. We had also advised him to consume more salt in his daily food. It had helped, but only a little. He looked particularly weak just then; his stomach had been empty since the night before, in preparation for the surgery, and he had been urinating even more frequently. When I looked at him carefully, I couldn't help feeling a strong surge of pity; he needed help even to get up.

Outside the hospital, it was an early summer day, beautiful, and full of hope. The first round of local-level elections was over, and thousands of Nepalese people were on their way to Bombay, Surat, Delhi and Shimla. The summer day instilled in them the hope that they'd make a better living in India; Nepal had nothing to give them. Many men and women were on their way to the airport to board a flight to Qatar. Even though, recently, as many as six Arab countries had broken their diplomatic ties with Qatar, it was now being embraced by Nepal. It would give the Nepalese children quality education in a private school. Of the people left behind, many were ascending the subalpine and alpine tundra in search of Yarsagumba, a magic aphrodisiac.

That day was showering challenges everywhere. People were acting on their impulses to seek a better life, doing what made them happy and brought them satisfaction. If only I had a way of satisfying my mental state, of quenching my thirst to seek answers!

Indeed, so many questions were unanswered. They kept me awake at night. How did Charles kill? What was his motive? Did his victims struggle? Did he have any remorse? Why did he come to Nepal?

All these questions could get answers—truthful, complete answers. But only if I tried a narco-test. A heavy dose of Diazepam and an injection of Ketamine could make him weak enough to answer anything he was asked. Neither his mind nor his body would be strong enough to concoct untruths or conceal anything whatsoever.

What was I thinking? It sounded horribly unethical to me, even as a mere thought inside my head. On many occasions, I had discussed with my colleagues the ethics of conducting a narco-test only to satisfy one's curiosity. I would always narrate the story of Vishwamitra in this context; he is one of the most revered sages in Hindu mythology. When he started his intense meditation, Lord Indra, the king of heaven, got frightened. The sage appeared set to create a new heaven for himself! He sent Menaka, the most beautiful apsara and celestial nymph to the earth. She successfully seduced Vishwamitra; he gave in to his temptation and dropped his penance. 'Temptation is evil,' I would declare grandly to my listeners. 'It makes you do bad things. We as doctors have to be above temptation.'

Well, I was no Vishwamitra. My profession didn't have the power to endanger heaven. They sometimes said surgery was little more than a series of 'Darbhanga scars'—the mere cutting and sewing of the skin. What could I say to that really? The Hippocratic oath, too, I had long found, was of no relevance. Even if I did give in to my temptation and performed a narco- test on Charles, nobody but my moral voice would question me.

Perhaps it was the best thing to do. Isn't it only fair—and smart—to do something a little murky if the larger goal is noble? A narco-test could help reveal the motive of a serial killer. It could help protect the lives of thousands of people

in the future. It could help the world put an end to brutality
for good.

*

My phone kept ringing all morning. Most of the callers 'hoped
Charles Sobhraj would die'. A few sent me best wishes. One
journalist couldn't contain his impatience. He left me messages
and called me a number of times before I picked up.

'How was the operation? Please tell me. Is it over yet?'

'His operation hasn't even started yet.' I tried to speak
as politely as possible. It was all I could do to keep myself
composed. Everyone had priorities. The journalist's mission in
life was the big story; my mission just then was finding some
answers.

*

Subita was displaying Charles's chest X-ray on the board. She
checked his armband and started writing the details on the
board. Not that she needed to check anything at all when this
patient was concerned; she knew everything about his case, like
the back of her hand.

Charles Sobhraj, 73 years, male.
Height: 161 cm, Weight: 71 kg.
Diagnosis: Severe mitral regurgitation with severe tricuspid
regurgitation.
Surgery: Mitral repair or replacement with tricuspid repair.

My patient had already been on Diazepam since the night before.
Ketamine too was running in his blood. The nurse opened a
cannula in his right arm and injected the requisite dose of
morphine. Now, he was as vulnerable as a baby. The drugs

would have worked rapidly to lull all his senses and make his mind a clean slate.

'Who are you?' I asked him, patting his arm softly.

Every single person in the room was looking at Charles with gimlet eyes. I think some of the people started recording the proceedings on their mobile phones.

'Charles Sobhraj. Charles Gurumukh Sobhraj,' he replied in a deep, throaty voice.

'What do you want?'

'I want to live.'

That did it. The Menaka dancing in my mind and distorting my clarity of thought fell, never to get up. I turned to the anaesthesiologist-in-charge, 'You can proceed.'

While washing my hands for the surgery, I felt a little more peaceful. I had not been carried away. Considering that my mind had been a whirlwind for several weeks now, this was quite a personal triumph. My suprarenal glands had perhaps decided not to inject any more adrenaline in my blood. My endless anxieties about the surgery and its outcome had ensured I already had enough.

Sandesh, one of my friends from the time I was training to be a surgeon, used to say, 'Even a monkey can be trained to be a surgeon.' Ironically, he later decided to be one of the primates himself—a plastic surgeon. Primate or not, I had operated on thousands of hearts in the last seventeen years and—even if it was only because of the practice—had developed a good amount of dexterity. I knew what to do with Sobhraj's heart; I just hoped it would be enough.

Sobhraj had been prepped and draped. His body had been attached to a ventilator, and there was an ultrasound probe through his gullet. I let Subita make the incision over his chest.

Ansu cut his sternum. Then, I cut through his heart sac with a diathermy pencil.

Eureka! I wanted to shout. I sure would have something to tell my wife later that day.

Inside the sac was Sobhraj's heart. A normal-looking, human heart. A heart beating innocently, oblivious to the monstrosities committed by the one it was beating for.

★

How is an open heart surgery performed? Strangely, it is rather simple. It was John Heysham Gibbon who developed and performed surgery with a heart-lung machine. Although that was sixty years ago, the concept has remained the same over time. Deoxygenated blood from the body is taken away to a machine, where carbon dioxide is extracted from it and replaced with oxygen. This oxygenated blood is pumped back to the systemic circulation, thereby bypassing the work of the heart and the lungs in a human body.

On the sonographic display, I could see the posterior leaflet of his mitral valve—the left-sided valve between the two chambers of the heart. The leaflet was prolapsing towards the atrium, creating a massive blood leakage whenever his heart contracted. The overly dilated left atrium was unable to cope with this enormous outflow. The result was that it all flowed back to the lungs, building a high pressure on the blood vessels to the lungs, and a subsequent backlog in the right-sided chambers. Hence, the dilation and the leak in the valve between the two chambers of the heart. I now understood the complete morphology.

'Okay, let's check.'

I put a few stitches on the aorta—the main vessel that

supplies oxygenated blood—and put a pipe there. I also put a few more pipes in the veins that drained deoxygenated blood to the right side of the heart. In no time, his heart was empty. But it was still beating.

The nurse had already connected a system to act as a support kidney and remove extra fluid from the body. 'Decrease your flow!' I instructed; his aorta was clamped, and we now had to administer medicines. The medicines that would stop his heart.

I have often teased new medical officers, 'Have you ever seen a person whose heart did not beat for half an hour but he still walked away, alive and kicking?'

They would look at me to confirm if I meant it, and then shake their heads. They hadn't yet witnessed a heart surgery.

'Well, in a couple of months, you will be well placed to bet on it with your friends. You will be able to tell them you have seen people whose hearts stopped beating for an hour but they walked away alive. You will make some good money.'

That's precisely what happens in a standard heart surgery of this nature—the heart stops beating for the duration of the operation. For the next 30 minutes, Charles's heart stopped beating too. Meanwhile, I repaired the left side of his heart first, then the right, my hands steady as they worked on his valves.

Heart surgery evokes mixed opinions in the medical fraternity. Once, an Austrian surgeon called Theodor Billroth had called it an 'act of prostitution', demanding that any surgeon who tried to stitch up a wounded heart be publicly shamed by his colleagues. Heart surgeons are considered megalomaniacs; they are people who can stop your heart and make it start beating again. There is a tendency among this community to display superiority over others, with some surgeons behaving like the head god among other lower gods. 'Do you also experience such grandiose feelings?' a school friend had asked me after I told him I was a heart surgeon. 'Do you feel more powerful than your fellow human beings?'

In my childhood, my father loved telling me the story of a nobleman called Ramdas. He was famous in his village for being kind and charitable. He would spend his entire morning praying to Lord Shiva. After his prayers, he would work hard on his farm. He never refused anyone who came seeking his help. Since Ramdas was also a good orator, he would talk convincingly to his fellow villagers, advising them on humility, the right way of living, and how to be thankful to the Almighty. In no time, the villagers started thinking of him as an avatar—god himself, born on earth in the guise of a human being. Ramdas loved this new honour, and even started believing it himself.

Lord Shiva did not like these feelings of deluded grandeur in someone he had believed to be his true devotee. He decided to teach Ramdas a lesson.

'Do you want to be a true god?' Shiva appeared in front of Ramdas one day, much to his shock and delight.

'Oh! My lord!' cried Ramdas. 'Yes. Yes!'

'*Tathastu!*' said Shiva. 'But remember, you can neither be invisible nor retract your blessings. Your blessing will end only with your death.'

But Ramdas hardly heard Shiva completely, so excited was he over the amazing new blessing. His mouth went dry. Had Shiva indeed appeared and blessed him or had it been a dream? He decided to test it.

'I wish for a glass of water,' said Ramdas carefully, weighing every word.

Bingo! A giant glass filled with murky seawater appeared in the air. Even though it was undrinkable, Ramdas was overwhelmed to see that his blessing was indeed real. He hadn't been dreaming.

'I want a quarter-sized glass of lukewarm, drinkable water to appear on the table,' he revised his wish. The water he gulped down from the magical glass that appeared was the sweetest he had ever tasted.

The news of his powers spread far and wide. People came to him from the nearby villages and far-flung towns, seeking his blessings. Some brought with them dead bodies of their loved ones, their sons and daughters who were no more, hoping he could revive them. Ramdas couldn't be indifferent to their tears, the kind man that he was. He blessed them with immortality. Pretty soon, he was blessing everyone who came to him with immortality. Chants of *'Swamiji ki jai ho, jai ho!'* continued with rising momentum as he kept reversing death and extending life. Within a few years, all of humankind was immortal. Then started the immortalization of animals—cows and monkeys, mosquitoes and cockroaches, mango trees and dolphins.

It was all very well for a while, but this utopia where no one ever died wasn't set to last. One day, the farmers thought, 'Why should we work hard in the burning sun and the biting cold if we won't die without food?' They stopped cultivating rice and wheat. Shopkeepers closed their shops as no one remained to produce food. No woodcutter was willing to cut trees, and there were no bricks. No one to collect cotton and weave. No cobblers, no people to build houses or roads. The world turned into a jungle where people had nothing to wear, nothing to read, nowhere to go, and virtually, nothing to do.

Moreover, since everyone was immortal now, they had no fear of god. They stopped visiting Ramdas. For months on end, he remained alone in his cave without a soul to talk to.

There, in his cave, aghast at the mess he had created, Ramdas experienced remorse like no one ever had. He had changed the beautiful world into an overcrowded, unlivable, pointless mess. Playing god isn't something he was good at; indeed, he had ruined everything the gods had lovingly built. 'I wish that I die right now,' uttered Ramdas, and breathed his last.

My father's story had always remained with me. We are technocrats with access to sophisticated machines and drugs that let us repair ailing hearts. We are not gods. The story of Ramdas and the occasional tragedy at the operation table kept me grounded. I tried my best, but I could not always save lives. I was a heart surgeon, not god, and every operation I conducted had me praying fervently for success.

'Sir, a Mr Deepak wants to talk to you. He is asking about Charles's surgery,' Sushila interrupted me again.

That dratted journalist. 'Just switch off my mobile.' Sushila put the phone on silent instead.

The surgery was still going on. Before I could put a ring on his heart, I had to make his valve competent. After thoroughly checking the left-sided chamber, I closed the left atrium and proceeded to the right-sided valve. I made a semicircular stitch and sealed it. It was now time to get his heart to start beating again. I slowly disconnected the heart-lung machine, and voila, his heart was pumping normally.

'Check it on TEE.' I watched as the technician fiddled with the display monitor of the transesophageal echocardiogram. Apurba, a well-known anaesthesiologist, was guiding the transesophageal ultrasonic probe through his gullet and stomach. Hold on; something was amiss. Apurba manoeuvred the probe from 0° to a 180° and saw it too.

Blood was still leaking through his left-sided valve. It wasn't much, yes, but it was definitely there.

I have to make a confession. If it had been any other person who had a leaking valve, I would have made another attempt at repair. Maybe a valve ring would have reinforced the surgery and fixed the leak completely. But it was a probability, not a certainty. Charles Sobhraj was not my regular patient; he was someone whose operation was being carefully tracked by the police, government authorities, and media outlets around the world. If even a minute leak persisted in his heart after the operation, it would raise a million questions on my ability (or the lack of it) as a surgeon. It had to be a one-time business, and it had to be thorough.

I started the bypass again, this time intending to uproot the cause of the problem. I was going to replace the faulty valve with a biological prosthesis. This time, it was more straightforward. I replaced his left-sided valve with a pericardial bio-prosthesis—C-E Perimount plus, size 31. Then, I closed his heart chambers and detached the heart-lung machine.

His heart started beating again. The sonogram did not reveal any malfunctioning.

'Close him,' I told Nivesh and rushed to another theatre where Nirmal was operating on a kid. He was waiting to patch a hole between the two chambers of the kid's little heart.

*

'He is doing well, Dai,' Apurba said to me when I returned. I sat down on the chair and drank three glasses of water.

10

BREAKING THE NEWS

The prime minister's herd of ministers had touched the magic number of hundred. But the news had not yet been published. Violent protests were going on in some nearby towns that wanted to negotiate a constitutional amendment in their favour. This too hadn't been printed. MS Dhoni still needed a couple of hundreds to make a front-page cover story in the Indian media.

But I was going to be in the news. Front page, no less. It shook me entirely out of gear.

On the day of the surgery, I had called my eldest brother before leaving for the hospital. As a psychiatrist, he usually had great advice. 'Daju![5] I need to talk.' In the silence of that morning, I could almost hear reporters rushing to the hospital.

---

[5]Nepali word for brother

Although very few media houses knew that the operation was scheduled for the day, do these stories remain quiet?

'What's up?' he asked casually, unaware of the turbulence going on in my life.

'I am struggling with two problems, Daju,' I began. I have always found it easy to talk to him. 'The first is that I have to operate on Charles Sobhraj today. How hard do you think the backlash will be if something goes awry?'

'Nothing will go wrong,' he said quietly.

'But you know, he is a deadly serial killer...'

'And he is your patient! It's part of your profession, so just proceed. That's what any cardiac surgeon in your place would have done. What are you worried about?' That's the usual way my brother talks—calm yet calculating, composed yet intuitive enough to grasp everything I felt and couldn't put in words.

'Okay. And here's my second problem—how should I break the news?'

'Gosh, you don't have to worry about that. Hundreds of journalists must have already gathered at Gangalal. They will break the news even if you don't!'

'So, you're saying it's okay if I avoid them altogether?'

'Of course, it will be fine. Best of luck!'

I mulled over what he said as I sipped my tea, trying to calm my nerves. Would the media let me be? Well, I had to hope.

It was past midday; I had finished my third operation. I went to the hospital cafeteria to grab a bite and sat there, eating momos in silence, gazing at old photographs on my phone. I chose a picture with him; it was one where we sat together, looking into the camera. My operating suit carried my name in Devanagari script, the script of Nepali—our national language—as well as of Hindi. I thought about the best caption for the news. What was the question Poonam had asked me over dinner, that night I had first told her I was taking up the case?

'Does he have a heart?'

Nothing could be better than answering this legit question, especially now that I had the verified answer.

I knew the news would be inundated with feedback—some of it positive, perhaps, congratulating me on the successful surgery. But most of it, I suspected, would be black. Condemnation for the brouhaha about a convict's medical treatment, that too, on government money. Anger against the happy picture that showed a doctor posing with a serial killer, his arm around the murderer's shoulder. Scorn directed at me for not letting journalists break the news. But I was mean then. Twitter was my blog, my newspaper. I could share anything I pleased on it and didn't have to give tuppence to naysayers.

I checked my call log. There were nearly twenty missed calls, some of them from people I knew. A few were repeat calls made in quick succession. Many people were waiting to know the outcome of the surgery. They deserved to hear it from the doctor who had performed it. Somehow, the missed calls reinforced my decision. It was my case, and I should be the one to share any details about it with the larger public. Was I selfish? I didn't stop to think. I finished the last momo and posted a tweet, attaching to it the chosen picture.

12 June 2017, Monday, 1:56 p.m.

Yes! He has a heart and I just fixed the valves inside. Recovering normally. #CharlesSobhraj

There, the deed was done. I shut the flap of my phone and headed to the next surgery scheduled for the day.

*

Inside the operation theatre, my phone was on silent again. But my mind was far from silent. On and off, random thoughts came into my head. Had people seen my tweet yet? How were people reacting to it? In my humdrum and low-profile life as a doctor in Nepal, stunts like these were novel. I was grateful that the present surgery was basic—it only took me a few minutes before Nivesh could take over.

In the surgeon's duty room, I sat drinking a cup of black tea. It was a quiet, secluded place; no one else was in the room. I resisted the urge to check my Twitter timeline; instead, I wondered if I had done the right thing. There was no denying that I had saved the life of a cold-blooded murderer, someone who had killed innocent people in revolting ways. Bloodbaths of any kind appalled me. Poonam still tried to shield me from news stories about the Maoist movement in Nepal—a movement I criticized vehemently for claiming nearly 17,000 lives. I had performed the surgery for reasons that couldn't possibly be contained in a tweet with a character limit. Why then did I break the news like that? Wouldn't it have been better to intimate the journalists instead?

I thought about a professor at my teaching hospital—a rather macho man and English scholar who had made a great impression on me. He rode an old Opel car which he had bought from the customs office during a store clearance bid for abandoned items. A hippie had deserted the car, and my professor gladly bought it, jumping into the driver's seat every morning, wearing a funky T-shirt and sunglasses. He would often tell us, 'As surgeons, you should know what is best for your patient. Be dedicated to the procedure, try your best to help the patient make a complete recovery, and then forget about the outcome. Anticipation is painful baggage. Leave it in the changing room with your dirty suits.'

That is what I tried to do. I went to check on my patients in the ICU and found that Charles was doing quite well. The bleeding was under control, and he was likely to gain consciousness soon. I left for home. On my way back, I did not check the comments on my tweet. The only engagement I made with the big news I had broken was texting an 'okay' to Ashok. He wanted permission to use the picture I had posted on Twitter.

Back home, I switched on my laptop to pen down a blog about the surgery. My thoughts were cooking up such a crazed storm that I felt I had to unleash them into the world. Writing would be a good way of doing that. By 8:00 p.m., I had published the blog. 'Today, I fixed the heart of a heartless man,' I wrote, sharing my experiences of the surgery. In a country where even minor celebrities rush abroad for medical treatment, doctors in Nepal are left with either no name or a bad name. But here was a celebrity—and not a minor one at that—who had trusted the Nepalese healthcare system with his life.

My mind offloaded, at least a little, I started browsing through my Twitter newsfeed and other news channels. Though I didn't talk to any journalist, all kinds of speculations were made.

KATHMANDU: A French serial killer, nicknamed the 'Bikini Killer' for a string of murders throughout Asia in the 1970s, is recovering after having open heart surgery in Nepal on Monday, his doctor said.

Charles Sobhraj, 73, currently serving a life sentence for two murders in Kathmandu in 1975, has undergone a five-hour surgery to repair the valves in his heart.

'The good news is that the operation was a success,' Sobhraj's wife Nihita Biswas told AFP.

It was a four-hour surgery, but they had to extend it for another hour because they found that the other valve was also damaged. Right now, they say, he's stable.

Raamesh Koirala—one of the three surgeons involved in the complicated procedure—said that Sobhraj would remain sedated for 24 hours. 'We cannot say he is out of danger until 24 hours go by, maybe longer. But the operation was successful,' said the surgeon, who is a distant relative of Biswas.

The ageing con man—who has been implicated in more than 20 killings—is under tight security in the hospital because of threats made against his life, his wife said.

Sobhraj is expected to remain in intensive care for at least four days.

Randeep Hooda: 'How did it go for #CharlesSobhraj?'

The news was flooded with Charles Sobhraj; the international media seemed even more excited than the local press. A handful had praised the effort, commending the success of the complicated surgery. But most people on social media seemed to think it was an act of insanity. Doctors are trained to be empathetic towards their patients, irrespective of their occupations—even if it was killing. But all that, it seemed, looks good only in books; in real life, I was being called the 'twin brother' of the serial killer. Someone had posted a meme titled 'Nepalese doctor discovers that Charles Sobhraj has a heart'. Someone from South Korea had drawn a cartoon featuring

Charles and me, surrounded by bikinis. The cartoon was swiftly becoming popular.

I learnt a big lesson that day; the media is not forgiving or generous. In recent times, Nepal had been through a lot. Birendra, the last king, had died in a royal massacre. The new king was suspected by many of having played a role in the bloodshed. But Nepal was still the 'Himalayan Kingdom' as far as the media was concerned. The sobriquet had more undercurrents of feudalism and primitiveness than spirituality. Our tourism ministry went on and on about how 'The Mt. Everest is in Nepal' and 'the Buddha was born in Nepal', but none of that gave us any standing in the world arena. The news about Charles's surgery was much the same. It made better sense for the media to focus on the con man, his family, and the ethics of the operation as compared to the medical challenges it had involved.

I felt no remorse. I was a heart surgeon by profession and had done what I had to. I would have done so even if Charles was set to be hanged to death the day after being discharged from the hospital. His case had been special to me, and I didn't find this feeling unreasonable. Every surgeon dreams of treating dignitaries, at least of his own country. The dream only gets magnified when you're talking about a country where nearly everyone with some money in the bank flies to New Delhi or Singapore for medical treatment. I had seen politicians enjoying a luxurious treatment in foreign hospitals even if their only complaint was a hernia in their groin. Charles Sobhraj could have done so too, but hadn't. Famous or infamous, he was the most well-known person in Nepal at that time. I saw no reason for remorse; I saw a legitimate reason for pride.

Poonam had heard about the surgery too. During dinner, I tried to show her some news clippings on my phone. But she refused.

'You know, just because you saw a physical, beating heart does not mean he *has* a heart. The soul does not reside here,' she said, patting the left side of her chest. 'It resides up there.' She pointed above her right ear. 'Without a soul to guide your heart, it is as good as burnt rubber.'

Perhaps she was right. Maybe Charles did have a heart, but it was black and dead, beating without a soul.

★

I was sitting in front of them with my hands tied tightly to a chair. Such things almost never happened in Kathmandu, at least not in broad daylight. I had been en route to the hospital when they crept up from behind, silent as death, and abducted me. They sat there now, glaring at me with scorn, filling the air with the stench of their sweat and marijuana.

'When will she come?' said an Asian man with a thick moustache. He had an Arabic accent.

'Connie told us to wait, dear,' replied a white woman, putting her arms around his shoulders and giving him a quick, consolatory kiss on the cheek. She was wearing a long shirt-dress, transparent enough to show the blue, floral bikini she had on underneath. A couple sat on my left, taking little interest in the proceedings.

'Henk, you are not here on a honeymoon trip. Start questioning him!' The man with the Arabic accent shouted at the couple.

Suddenly, the door opened, and another white woman walked into the room. Her face was stern; water droplets clung to her body almost as if she was directly coming from a pool.

'Did he say anything? Show any remorse?' The woman, the picture of fury, scanned everyone's face. She met my eyes too. In her right hand, she brandished something that I, despite myself, couldn't help but call a whip. A whip with glistening metal near the tail.

'We haven't asked him yet,' Henk responded, clutching his girlfriend's hands tightly.

'Of course, you haven't. You are just a vleesroos lover.'

Thrash! The whip pierced through the thick air in the quiet room, a few sparks gleaming from its tail momentarily. Henk's girlfriend put her hand over her mouth, trying hard to suppress a scream. He rubbed the small of her back and stroked her hair, doing everything he could to calm her down.

Connie then spoke to me directly. 'So, doctor, tell me why you did it. Why did you prolong our wait? What was in it for you?'

'Sorry? What wait?'

She made an irritated noise. 'Don't pretend to be innocent. You doctors know the easiest, most ruthless way to kill people, don't you?'

That did make sense. I had read somewhere that if a doctor transforms into a murderer, he can choose smart and almost undetectable ways to kill. I nodded.

She grabbed a fistful of my hair. 'Tell me, do you think it is easy to die when someone drowns you, forcefully keeping your head under the water? Is it easy to be burnt alive?'

I was in considerable pain as she tightened her hold over my hair, pulling a few hairs out and digging her nails into my skin. 'No,' I managed to say.

'Then why did you do it? Why did you prolong our revenge? You traitor!'

I gathered all the courage I had and asked her, 'Who are you? Why am I here?'

She didn't answer. No one answered. In front of my eyes, she transformed into Kali, the fiercest deity of Hindu mythology, and danced with her whip in a manner so sinister that my entire body was drenched in sweat.

'For the last forty years, we have been waiting to seek revenge. And now, you have saved our killer. You must pay for it!'

She whirled her lash again, aiming straight in the direction of my neck. Before it could hit me, my eyes snapped open, and I screamed into the night.

I couldn't get a wink of sleep after that nightmare and sat by the window from midnight until the wee hours of the morning. It was only when dawn dispelled the darkness that some of the horrors in my heart disappeared. I couldn't help shake my head at the opposing forces of the universe. There was someone in the hospital, recovering from a dangerous medical procedure and praying for life. And there were people in my nightmares desperately waiting for his life to end.

11

THE QUEST FOR THE ANSWER

The next morning, I drove my car to the hospital. It was only a ten minutes stroll from my home, but I didn't want to give the nightmare any chance to realize itself. I was getting sick of nightmares; I was also getting scared of them. Ever since that phone call at Khaptad, nightmares had never left me. And the horror fest of the night before only proved that things were getting worse. Was there something wrong with me? What was I afraid of? Perhaps, I concluded, it was merely my confusion and anguish about saving the life of someone who had taken dozens of lives. It was a terrible struggle between Raamesh, the human being, and Raamesh, the doctor.

Many hippies used to say that Kathmandu changed them in subtle but overpowering ways. When they started their journey from London or Paris, they were mere tourists. But after reaching Kathmandu, they transformed into travellers—

people with a keen interest in the culture and life of the local inhabitants. But that morning, the traveller I was checking in on did not seem the least bit interested in the world around him. He lay there, reclined on the bed, demanding more opioids for the pain.

Meanwhile, Nepal was busy trying to find new ways to free itself of Indian supremacy. For decades, Nepalese politicians had blamed our southern neighbour for the deceleration in our development. Most of the time, it was merely a ploy to hide their ineptitude. But recently, things had taken a turn for the worse. The Bengal government had brutally suppressed the protests organized by Nepali speaking people in the eastern hills of India. The Narendra Modi government did not seem interested in improving ties with Nepal.

The social sentiment, too, was becoming anti-Indian, which accelerated after the recent economic blockade. Ever since Hrithik Roshan, a Bollywood actor, had allegedly run down Nepalese people, the cinemas had stopped screening his movies for a long time. The cinemas were used to facing boycotts like these; the same thing had happened for another Indian actor— Dharmendra. It was such a time that even if some primary schoolteacher in Kerala had apparently claimed that the Buddha was an Indian, it would still be enough fodder to start the fire of mass protest in Kathmandu—a three-day nationwide shutdown with deaths and assaults, the victims mainly poor barbers and vegetable vendors from North India. So strong was the anti-Indian sentiment in the country that people heartily cheered the 'One Belt One Road' agreement Nepal signed with China. The foreign minister had also given his approval to a Chinese company for a 1200MW hydropower project in the Budhi Gandaki River.

The German ambassador, too, was having an eventful time. He was on the hippie trail, planning to drive through India, Pakistan, Iran, Turkey, Greece, Macedonia, Albania, Croatia, Italy and Austria, to finally reach Germany. During the era of 'The Overland', the bygone days of the hippie trail, Macedonia and Croatia didn't even exist. He stopped briefly at Lumbini—a Buddhist pilgrimage site in Nepal—and the media picked up the incident with great enthusiasm. It didn't take much to make Nepal proud; feelings of grandeur emanate from just about the smallest of triumphs when you have been used to prolonged oppression and negligence from the rest of the world. At any chance for a morale boost, we started dancing in joy, claiming that, of course, Nepal was a *great* country and it had been set back only because of conniving neighbours. The Buddha was born in Nepal, wasn't he?

Trapped in the conflicts of my mind, I was relatively shielded from all the uprisings for national pride. By midnight that day, Charles was detached from the ventilator. We continued a small dose of catecholamine to support his recovering heart.

On my regular rounds of the ICU later that night, I saw Charles sleeping. On an impulse, I went close to him and patted him softly on the shoulder. He woke up instantly and looked at me with half-open eyes, crinkles appearing on his forehead.

I knew he was still under the effect of Fentanyl, an opioid, but I couldn't help myself. If it was a misuse of my powers, so be it. *'Aankha khola ta,'* I asked him to open his eyes, speaking in a soft voice.

He obeyed, opening his eyes properly and parting the curtains to see me better. I had always known that he understood the Nepali language. I had tried several times to get him to react to Nepali before, but this was the first time he humoured me.

His face did not give away any emotion; it was blank.

'Did you get a call from Reik?' he asked me in English.

'No.'

Charles looked disappointed. Reik was, supposedly, a TV reporter from London. A day before the operation, Charles had given me a piece of paper with two phone numbers—Reik's and that of a female reporter from New Delhi, a friend of Charles. 'They will call you after the surgery,' he had assured me. But no call had come yet. Or perhaps they had called me when my mobile had been switched off.

'If they do call, tell them I am fine.'

I nodded absent-mindedly; I wasn't paying attention to his demands but struggling with the voices in my head. 'Sir, let's ask him about his deeds!' squealed Subita in my head. 'You'll not get a better chance than this,' said someone else, sounding a lot like me. There were tons of questions longing to be asked; they were sure to be answered as Charles was under the influence of Fentanyl. Even his brutal, conniving mind could not lead him out of the haze that morphine induces in the brain.

'Did you kill the American backpacker, Connie Jo Bronzich? What about her friend Laurent Carriere?'

'Why did you commit such brutal murders?'

'Why did you return to Nepal when you knew this was the only country with active charges of murder against you?'

'What was your motive?'

'Who *are* you?'

I did not ask any of those questions; I couldn't bring myself to.

But every day, the questions kept increasing in number and growing in intensity. Not only Subita but other junior doctors also had questions of their own. The ICU nurses gossiped. Hushed conversations were everywhere. I would go to check his condition every day, charting the course from ICU bed number 4 to deluxe cabin number 2. Every day, I would go through his medical records, answer any questions he had, and ensure his vital statistics were normal.

'How do you feel today?' was the only question I ever voiced.

★

'What's the matter?' Poonam asked me one night. Every night after coming back from the hospital, I had taken to sitting on the balcony and drinking my Carlsberg. I would stare at the night sky for hours, unable to participate in anything.

'Nothing special,' I answered. What was I to tell her? I could tell her, perhaps, that I was upset about Dhoni's recent performance. He had had two chances to bat in the ICC Champions Trophy, but he had only made 67 runs. The dream of a thousand ODI runs was as far away as the stars I had been watching. But I did not tell her that; it would have only reinforced her suspicion that her husband had some sort of psychological disorder.

I chose, instead, to give her a vague answer.

★

For the last twenty years, I had been a practising physician. I had an aspiration to lift the face of the public health sector in Nepal and salvage it from the murk of the political labyrinth. I used to dream of building an exemplary government heart centre with facilities at par with those in private institutions. But that dream had long died.

One of my dreams persisted—the dream to be a writer. A

novelist. Perhaps a member of the World Union of Physician-Writers. Be as famous as Khaled Hosseini and Taslima Nasreen. I had published two books by then and received some recognition in the Nepalese literature circle. But it was only a beginning, a candle to the fire of my dreams.

'It is good to dream,' my father used to tell me. 'Dreams should have no end.' And so I dreamed on. I dreamed of being an op-ed writer, a journalist, the voice of commoners. But above all, I dreamed of being an interviewer.

On nights when I wasn't afflicted by nightmares, I would sometimes dream of Lord Buddha. In my dream, I'd be interviewing him. 'Did you ever get a Nepalese citizenship?' I would ask him. I am still clueless why I chose that question from the ocean of questions I could have posed to the Buddha. I also dreamed of interviewing Tenzing Norgay, asking him about his citizenship. The logic behind this question, however, was clear in my head. I wanted to know whether our pride in singing, '*Hamro Tenzing Sherpa le chadyo himal chuchura*'[6]—a celebratory song for the Nepalese mountaineer—was justified or not.

The interview dreams I loved most were those involving Manisha Koirala, a beautiful Bollywood actress. She would talk about riding her horse, describing how she had fallen off the horse, and I would nearly fall off my chair too. She would describe her journey of fighting ovarian cancer, and I would find my eyes welling up.

For the last few days, however, my dreams had been monopolized by only one person—Charles Sobhraj. I dreamed

---

[6]A poem roughly translated as 'Our Tenzing Sherpa has concurred Peak of the Himalayas'.

of sitting in front of him with a pen and paper, asking questions one after the other, quenching the thirst that had haunted me ever since Charles had first entered my life on that Khaptad trip.

But when I would wake up in the morning, the dream would seem far too frightening.

★

The lights were too bright, almost harsh. The cameras were ready, but the technicians kept fiddling with them. A little to the left, a little to the right. Talk shows involved too much preparation, even though the audience probably thought they were the simplest television programme to produce. All you needed was a host, a celebrity, and a cup of coffee! But never mind all that, the interview was surely worth it.

Dr Raamesh had taken a lot of convincing. He kept making excuses for not letting me interview Charles Sobhraj. 'He is still in the intensive care unit,' my alter ego would declare, refusing the interview point-blank. Sometimes he would say, 'He is still on morphine.' As if that mattered! But here it finally was. The dais was set in my dreamscape, and Alain Gauthier sat, ready to be interviewed.

'Good morning, Mr Alain. How are you?'

'I am fine. Recovering from the heart surgery,' Alain's voice was soft with a hint of a French accent—his trademark style.

'So, Alain, you've been serving your sentence in a hundred-year-old jail, right in the heart of Kathmandu. How has your experience been?'

'Horrible,' he scowled. 'Pathetic and inhuman.'

'What? But the documentaries show that you were having a good time even inside the prison.'

'How can you trust those things? I am constantly kept in

isolation. It has been an eternity. Are you aware that such solitary confinement is against the Nepalese law?'

'Well, but you do have access to the Internet and also possess a mobile phone. Is that so?'

'I had to bribe a lot of people to get that. It's not part of the system,' he said this without flinching, but I could see his face turn a little red.

'You managed to break out of Tihar. But the Central Jail in Kathmandu seems to be unbreakable. Don't you think it is ruining your reputation? The reputation of a serpentine?'

He kept quiet. I repeated the question. 'What do have to say?'

'I'm not a serpentine,' he spat. 'Mind your language, doctor.'

'I'm not a doctor.'

'Oh, sorry! It's just that you look a lot like him.'

'It's okay. You resemble someone else too.'

He deigned to laugh before I continued. 'Do you think a lack of motive has something to do with it? You had a motive for your jailbreak in India. But now you've given up?'

'No sweat. I will be free in a few days. The Supreme Court has no evidence against me. As soon as I get a hearing, I will be free.'

I glanced at my sheet of paper and read out the next question. I sensed that the interview was going to be a big hit. 'Were you ever a hippie?'

'No, never. I have always lived a good life. Until now in Nepal, that is.'

'Okay, so you were not a hippie. What did you do in India then?'

'I was in car trade. Those hippies sold their cars at a very low price. I used to sell these abandoned cars. It was a business with a good margin.'

'What about your business in Bangkok? Did you sell cars there too?'

'The car trade turned out to be less profitable, so I choose to begin dealing in gems. Since Bangkok is close to Burma, it was the ideal location for that business.' He sure had an answer to every question, fairly convincing ones at that.

'Mr A Guthier, Kanit House, Apt. 504, 77/5, Soi Salasaeng, Bangkok. Was this your address there?'

'It might have been. It was a long time ago.'

'It seems you were in Kabul for some time. In Goa and Delhi too. Didn't you ever visit Kathmandu for your business?' I couldn't help place some extra emphasis on the 'business'.

'No. I had never been to Kathmandu.'

'So, 2003 was the first time you came here?'

'That's what I have constantly been repeating in court.'

I figured he wasn't going to tell me the truth, I was searching. I changed the subject. 'How has your recovery been? Are you gaining strength at the hospital?'

'You know, my first daughter was born in Breach Candy. Even that was better than this.'

'You mean, in Mumbai?'

'Yes.'

His relaxed, considered responses were putting me off. *To hell with your entire family*, I wanted to scream. *I am not here to compare hospitals or know your pedigree*. I decided to be direct; I had had enough of the beating around the bush.

'Do you feel any remorse? Any at all?'

'For what?'

'For the murders? The brutal murders you committed?'

For a moment, I thought he'd say, 'I have never killed good

people.' But he was silent.

'Why did they arrest you in Kathmandu?'

'Bloody Knippenberg!' he declared, throwing his arms up in the air. 'It was his bribes that did it!'

◆

12

CHARLES, MY RELATIVE

I saw her on Monday afternoon, the day of the surgery. It was my usual practice to discuss my surgeries with the family members of the patients. It helped them understand the situation thoroughly and get prepared for future precautions and check-ups. Many family members turned up for these discussions, and the hospital was continually running short of space to seat them all. While some accommodated themselves in the common lobby, ten trying to fit in a bench made for five, others made do with the marble floor.

I opened the door at the end of the corridor and called out, 'Charles Sobhraj!'

I was expecting to see five police officers, and probably a worried lady possessing a small frame—his lawyer. Instead, a young girl with a healthy glow on her face ran towards me. I recognized her instantly, possibly from the scandalous television programmes and her stint on *Bigg Boss*. It was Nihita Biswas.

She didn't look much like her mother, except that she too had a small stature. She was dusky and big-eyed, and exuded a distinct Bengali aura. Numerous pairs of eyes looked up as she started running; I could almost feel their ears straining to hear the conversation between us.

I addressed her in a low voice. 'His surgery was successful. I tried to repair the valve, but it did not work out well. I had to replace it since his heart was too frail to withstand a continued leak and the prospect of another surgery in the future.'

Tears rolled down from her eyes.

'Don't worry; he is doing fine now. He needs to remain in the hospital for a few days, but he has started recovering.'

'When will he wake up, doctor?'

'After heart surgeries, nearly all patients need to remain sedated in the ICU. We stop the sedatives only after checking that everything is normal. So, it will depend on how quickly he recovers.'

She nodded slightly and walked back to her seat, her face directed away from me.

That evening, of all the news reports I saw, there was one that caught me completely off guard. *The Telegraph*, a news agency based out of the United Kingdom, had this curious quote:

> We did not want the surgery to happen in Nepal because we do not trust Nepal. That is why we got hold of a doctor who is related to the family. We could trust only a relative with the surgery.

What? Me, a relative of Charles Sobhraj? I had never known that my ancestors had visited Indo-China; Sobhraj's parents had never visited Nepal. There hadn't even been an inter-caste marriage in my extended family. Exactly how were Charles and I related?

I called Gyanmani Mama. His curious connection with Charles had left me stumped that day in Khaptad. Perhaps he would know something? 'Mama, how is Charles my relative?' I asked him over the phone. 'Nihita told a British news agency that I am related to his family.'

Mama chuckled. 'I am afraid I have something to do with it. You know that I have known Shakuntala Didi for a long time, don't you? Well, I had a college senior called Biswas in Bhadrapur, who later got married to her. Their daughter studied in the same school as my cousin; she used to call me uncle.'

★

The morning news was flooded with pictures of Tribhuvan International Airport; a huge amount of gold had been seized there again. I wondered how someone repeatedly dared to smuggle hundreds of kilograms of gold via the airport. A friend once told me, 'Those kilos of gold amount to nothing. The real stuff—thousands of kilos, not hundreds—are smuggled through customs.' Perhaps Charles's confidence of being able to smuggle an elephant through Nepalese customs wasn't just bravado.

Charles was now fit enough to be transferred to his cabin. The swelling from his legs had already vanished; his lungs were as dry as the roasted coffee beans I had beaten for my morning cup. His kidneys were producing a fairly good amount of urine on their own, and we had stopped the diuretics. Catecholamines were not needed anymore to boost the pumping of his heart. We kept him in the ICU a little longer than required, mainly because the hospital could not afford separate nurses for all the patients in wards and cabins. But by the third day in the ICU, he was wide awake and flirting with some of the nurses. Or so they claimed.

'Why don't you have bedside tables here?' Charles enquired while I was completing his check-up.

'You mean these?' I pointed towards the bedside table on his left.

'No, no. I mean those tables to help you eat when you're in bed.'

'Oh, over-bed tables? Well, we do have some, but they are usually occupied by medical charts and X-rays. Whenever you need one, feel free to ask for it.'

He didn't look satisfied. 'Your ICU is quite good, and the staff is efficient. But these tables are not good.'

No one acknowledged that remark, but he went on nonetheless.

'How many beds do you have in the ICU?'

'Thirty-six.'

'Okay, then I will ask my embassy to donate thirty-six nice tables to the hospital.'

His embassy indeed! He talked as if he was the chief of the French embassy, overwhelming a small-time hospital with a massive act of generosity. It made me angry. Here was this European passport holder pretending to be a big shot when he possessed no more than two pairs of clothes and a single pair of colourless, torn shoes! I could never stand it when anyone treated our hospital and us like beggars.

'Rosy,' I called out to the nurse-in-charge. 'Give him a pair of slippers to wear. We can consider it a donation from the hospital to a French national. Or you can ask the accounting department to deduct the cost from my salary.'

Charles didn't seem to mind my angry, sarcastic remark. 'Did Reik call you?'

'No! I have already told you ten times. Why do you want these journalists to contact me anyway?'

'Many people want to know about my condition. I need to assure them that I'm fine.'

Of course. The world had almost stopped because they hadn't heard directly from a convict for some days. In any case, the media had already concocted detailed reports on his condition, even if they hadn't had a chance to verify most of them.

'What is the news outside?' he asked, looking interested. Keeping abreast of the news and being *in* the news was critical to him.

I could tell him that Pakistan beat India in the final of the ICC Champion's trophy; Dhoni had been able to score only four runs. I could also tell him that the BJP had nominated Mr Kovind, a scheduled-caste politician, as the presidential candidate. It was being seen as an excellent move by the Modi government. But I knew this was not the news he actually wanted to hear.

'Nothing special. Don't worry, the world knows about your surgery.'

'But I would like to tell everyone about my progress personally,' he declared as if a huge fan-following was waiting outside the hospital to meet him, eager to hear his voice and see his face.

'Okay,' I said, desperate to end the pointless, frustrating conversation. 'Let me do you a favour.' I took out my mobile phone and filmed a small video clip of about 30 seconds. Charles happily announced that he was doing well and recovering in the hospital. That evening, I uploaded the video on my Twitter account with the hashtag #CharlesSobhraj.

By the next morning, Randeep Hooda had quoted my tweet, saying that he was so glad to see him and hear about him, and was 'happy that it all went well'. There were two love emojis.

'No one else?' asked Charles, when I showed him the tweet.

I couldn't believe how self-absorbed he was. Was he expecting a flood of well-wishers to send him 'get well soon' messages? I am sure he wouldn't have liked the tone of the messages that *had* come in—words bathed in disgust, targeted against the both of us.

I ignored his question. 'How is your pain?' I asked instead. 'Are you still asking for morphine?'

'It's better. I haven't asked for morphine in the last two days.'

'Sir, when should we transfer him to the ward?' Rosy asked me in Nepali. We both knew that he understood Nepali well, but he didn't show any hint of recognition.

'He has already overstayed in the ICU. Charles, tomorrow, I am planning to send you to your ward.'

Sobhraj looked at me and nodded.

★

'Only two months are left, guys! We should start planning our trek as well as our physical training. I don't want to repeat what happened last time,' Comrade said. He had had called us for a meeting at Tabela, our favourite restaurant. A large trekking map of the Annapurna Circuit was spread on the table, kept in place by mugs of beer. It had been a long time since Khaptad, and we were now ready to embark on our next mission. Subry had renamed our Twitter group to 'Thorang-La aspirants'. I thought it had a nice ring to it.

Comrade had brought someone along to the meeting, someone I didn't recognize, but Subry seemed to know him quite well. 'Meet Suraj Shakya, Dai,' Subry introduced him to me. 'Though he won't be with us during our trek, he will guide us.'

Suraj, it seemed, had a lot of experience in high-altitude trekking. He spoke confidently about the best routes to take. 'If you are planning to ride a jeep, go up to Upper Pisang only. From there, take this route to Ghyaru and onwards to Ngawal,' he moved his index finger across the map as he spoke.

'Why not drive right up to Mugje?' I could not see the rationale behind walking half the day instead of riding in a four-wheeled jeep for two hours.

'If you ride, you won't be able to get a good look around. From Ghyaru, the view of the Annapurna-II is breathtaking. Of course, it's just a suggestion.'

'Let me write it down.' Subry started finalizing the itinerary we had roughly prepared on a piece of paper.

'Can I ask you something?' said Suraj. 'Why are you going to Mugje instead of the Upper Manang?'

'One of my patients has a hotel there. He wants us to stay at his hotel; it's a treat.'

'Oh, okay. So, on the first day, you will stay at Chame, 2,670 metres away. Then, on the next day, you will drive up to Upper Pisang, up to 3,300 metres, and start walking. You will reach Ghyaru, 3,670 metres far, in about three hours where you can have a late lunch. Then, it will be another two-hour trek to Ngawal, which is another 3,660 metres away...'

As I listened to Suraj's narration of the route, as fluent as if he had it memorized, I was struck by the varied geography up in the mountains. Every place on our high-altitude trekking route, it seemed, had a suffix in metres. I wondered how a map of the overland trail would look like if someone were to use a similar format. It would probably say Kandahar 2 Euro, Lahore 2.15 Euro, Goa 3.50 Euro, and Kathmandu 3.10 Euro—the suffix denoting the price of an ounce of black gum.

Within one hour, our itinerary was finalized. 'Remember,' warned Suraj, 'you have to start serious hiking practice before embarking on this circuit.'

But by now, most of the group was tired of talking about trekking. Comrade was bursting to ask me about the man who had fascinated him ever since that time in Khaptad.

'Is it true that his wife's blood is inside him?' Sometimes, I thought Comrade was even more updated with the latest news about Charles Sobhraj than me, the doctor who met him every day. His most recent question referred to a news report from Tanzania that had made him curious, even though he didn't 'exactly know' where Tanzania was.

'It's a lie. Nihita had donated her blood, but he didn't need it.'

'Does she know about this? The news report said that her blood was running through his body.'

'The news reporter probably had nothing better to write about,' I grimaced. 'Our hospital sends any remaining blood to the central blood bank unless someone asks for it to be returned to them. How can we possibly give bags of blood to people?'

★

Meanwhile, life in Nepal continued rapidly outside the hospital doors. After the 'One Belt One Road' deal with China, the Nepalese Army had started working hard to connect Kathmandu with Kerung, the Chinese border. It was going to be the fastest route to China. By 2020, the government planned to start a railway track from Xigaze to Kerung and Nepal was planning to bring it down to the capital. The pro-China sentiment contrasted sharply with the anti-Indian sentiment that continued to rise in the highlands. When Mamata Banerjee's government shut down Internet services in the Bengal hills, responding to constant

Gurkha agitation, the sentiment only became stronger.

Inside the hospital, however, things were quiet. Charles Sobhraj was recovering well, resting in his deluxe cabin and not taking the slightest interest in anything that didn't concern him. On a morning round one day, I checked his progress report. He weighed nearly ten kilograms less than he had at the time of admission. While major surgeries were sure to impact the body, a loss of ten kilograms was rather drastic.

'What is this?' I asked the nurse. His daily intake chart read: Bread, lychee, water, Coke, lychee, bread, lychee, chicken chowmein and lychee. 'What is with all that lychee?'

'He eats lychee all the time, doctor. I don't know why.'

I raised my eyebrows at Charles. 'Why do you eat so many lychees?'

'I can't help it, doctor,' he smiled. 'Back in my country, there were dozens of varieties of lychee. I would long to eat them all.'

'You mean in France?'

'No, Vietnam. Lychees originated there.'

'Really? I thought lychees originated in China.'

'China, Indo-China, India…' He smiled again and trailed off.

I glanced at his reports again. 'Okay, Charles. How are you doing?'

'I am fine now, doctor. But in the morning, I was feeling a little light-headed. It felt like my mind was floating somewhere in the sky.'

'Are you sure you weren't just longing for the feeling you must have been missing for a while?' Perhaps it was mean of me to hint at his days of drug use, but I couldn't help it.

Charles stared at me blankly. 'What?'

'I thought weed also induced a similar light-headedness.'

'Oh. I don't know; I have never tried drugs. I have never even smoked cigarettes. I hate people who do drugs.' He sounded bitter but not untruthful. I marvelled at the élan with which he could lie. I vividly remembered the Indian movie *Main Aur Charles* where Randeep Hooda smoked all the time.

I let it pass. What could I say or do, anyway, that would have the slightest impact on him? I finished my examination and removed the pacing wires attached to his chest wall. I was about to leave when he called out, 'Doctor! My embassy sent me this for speedy recovery. Can I eat it?'

In his hand was a bottle containing what I thought was pickle. Ah, liver pieces preserved in oil.

'No, don't eat it. Liver can alter the effect of the blood-thinning medicines you're on.'

I left him in his bed, staring at me with disappointed and somewhat disbelieving eyes.

★

In those days, apart from Charles Sobhraj, our upcoming trek also kept me busy. Sudeep Pokharel, a member of the Thorang-La aspirants, regularly shared advice for fitness training. He shared a 'small' post on the group—a post almost as big as an article—detailing everything we would need. Three layers of clothing, duffel bags, jackets, trekking poles, the works.

'What are trekking poles?' Comrade asked.

'Walking sticks, of course!' Sudeep often put on that officious tone, as if surprised beyond belief that we didn't know the professional names of trekking equipment.

As I got my bag ready, complete with trekking poles, Subry asked me something that drained all thoughts but one from my mind.

'Dai, when do you discharge your son-in-law?'

13

THE SERPENTINE IS FINALLY CAUGHT

Some mornings with Charles were easier than the others, mornings when he seemed more approachable and my mental dilemmas less intense. On one such day, I happened to ask him about his arrest in Nepal. It was something that had baffled me for long. Did the government of Nepal have enough proof to incriminate him for two murders? How had they arrested him?

'Ask my lawyer,' Charles replied. 'She will give you the details of the court hearings.'

Promptly, on her next visit to the hospital, Shakuntala brought along copies of the final judgement of the Kathmandu District Court and Charles's plea to the Human Rights Committee of the United Nations.

I am not a legal expert. But as I sat at my desk, reading the court papers, one thing was apparent even to me. Something was fishy.

✱

On 13 September 2003, Mr Rajesh Gurung, a young photojournalist at *The Himalayan Times*, had received an assignment from his editorial team—to get a photograph of Charles Sobhraj. The serial killer had been spotted at Thamel, and the newspaper was keen to get pictorial evidence.

From 14 to 16 September, Rajesh hung around the Thamel area, observing everyone closely. On the third day, his manhunt came to an end. He clicked several snaps of Charles Sobhraj, keeping his camera in stop-motion to capture every second of Charles's exit from the communication centre in Thamel.

On 17 September, a front-page news story appeared in *The Himalayan Times. Annapurna Post*, another newspaper from the same publishing house, also picked it up.

> The man known the world over as 'The Serpent' has come calling to Kathmandu. Charles Sobhraj, the internationally well-known ex-criminal and now a free man, has been camping in Thamel for the last fortnight. The ostensible reason for his visit is that he is attempting to forge ties with Nepalese entrepreneurs to export pashmina and possibly start a mineral water factory.

Three days later, on 20 September, the two newspapers ran another story about Sobhraj. This time, it was not as positive about the man's business plans.

> The man who once pompously claimed that he could smuggle in an elephant through the customs check at

Tribhuvan International Airport is today cooling his heels in the regional police office, Bhrikutimandap. Ironic as it may seem, Charles Sobhraj Gurumukh, known worldwide as 'The Serpent', was arrested from a local casino late last night by a special team of the Kathmandu Police.

The team, headed by Deg Bahadur GC, the deputy superintendent of police at the Valley Crime Investigation Branch, zeroed in on Sobhraj after a painstaking search spread over three days. The manhunt began on Wednesday when *The Himalayan Times* and *Annapurna Post* broke the story about Sobhraj being in Kathmandu. Following the report, the police began searching in hotels in Thamel and the Naya Bazaar area. They learnt that Charles had hired a room in The Garden Hotel in Naya Bazaar, but eventually found the room to be empty. The police then began looking in the casinos. He was apprehended by the police when he was having dinner at the casino and thereafter taken to the Kathmandu District Police Office.

That day, the international media had been flooded with the breaking news. Speculations had been endless. After all, Charles Sobhraj had been arrested in Nepal from the Royal Casino, from the very heart of the capital city of Kathmandu. What had he been doing there? Had he intentionally come back to Nepal to get arrested for murders committed 30 years ago? Or was the whole thing a mistake?

20 September 2003. Early in the morning, Charles was taken to the immigration department with an initial charge of passport forgery. The police prepared a case against him for entering the Nepalese territory with two different passports—one Dutch and the other French. He appeared in public later that day, covering

his face with a red handkerchief as the police dragged him to the Kathmandu District Court.

It was widely believed that the police was keeping him in custody for further investigation under the Immigration Act of Nepal. But the truth was different. Mr Baral, the deputy inspector general who headed the Valley Police Office, divulged the details to the media in a press conference. He said that the police department was not able to interrogate him properly due to the three-day national strike. The department was working on finalizing a charge sheet against him, a charge sheet much more serious than passport forgery. 'He is guilty of committing premeditated murders of two foreign nationals in Nepal,' said Mr Baral. 'He cannot escape the law anymore.'

'Mr Charles Sobhraj, what do you have to say about your arrest?' The journalists fell over each other as they tried to get an interview with Charles, even as the police pushed him inside the van.

'This is my first visit to Nepal. I have not committed any murders in Nepal.'

The police van sped out of the exit gate of the Kathmandu District Court, leaving his words and his conviction hanging in the air.

★

Later that day, the police remanded him, not entertaining any of his justifications or demands. For an entire month, they were busy preparing a charge sheet against him. From time to time, the police happily shared some of their findings with the media—and the public. If they took delight in grilling him about the murders he had committed, they did not hide it. The police unearthed it all, one by one.

The twin murders in 1975, a case investigated by Mr Chandra Bir Rai, then Superintendent of Police.

Illegal entry into Nepal in the guise of Dutch National Henricus Bintanja, using a passport with the identifier 'S 428929'.

Lying to the police about his previous visit to Nepal.

'I have never visited Nepal before this,' he insisted every day. 'I only came here now, in 2003, to start a business in handicrafts and pashmina.' But the police was not having any of that.

20 October 2003. The hearing began in the Kathmandu District Court. The charge sheet that the police had prepared with so much labour now showed two crimes—passport forgery and the murder of Connie Jo Bronzich. Initially, a few hearings took place in the court of Judge Mahara; the judiciary system of Nepal had a lottery system to decide the judge for each hearing. However, while the legal proceedings were going on, the judiciary system went through an amendment. Now, instead of assigning hearings via a lottery system, it was decided that all the hearings of one case would be led by one judge. It was believed that this system would speed up the process of meting out justice as well as help the judges develop expertise in a particular field. Judge Bishwombhar Prasad Shrestha was appointed Charles's judge. In one of the hearings, he dismissed the cases of passport forgery and illegal entrance to Nepal, as long back as in 1975, Nepal didn't have a relevant law covering this transgression.

12 August 2004. It was a Thursday, almost the end of the work week. Also, the day of the final verdict at the Kathmandu District Court. A huge crowd waited both inside and outside the premises, betting against each other, competing with the next person to break the most compelling news story on the verdict. The hearing started at 11:00 a.m., and Surya Nath Adhikari, the

Deputy Attorney, presented his case.

In 1975, claimed the attorney, Charles Sobhraj entered Nepal as a Dutch national called Henricus Bintanja. He stayed at Hotel Soaltee and then later joined his friends at Hotel Malla. He masqueraded around as a gem dealer, befriending hippies and spinning yarns. On 21 December that year, he hired a white Datsun car with the registration number 'B.A. 5001' from Gorkha Travels and Tours. The very next day, he stabbed—and then burned—Connie Jo Bronzich near the Manahara Bridge in Kathmandu. She was still alive when the flames engulfed her. On 23 December at 8:30 a.m., he flew to Bangkok aboard a Royal Nepal Airlines flight and returned the next day using the passport of Laurent Carriere, a Canadian national. The attorney stressed that Charles's crimes were heinous and unpardonable, and that, under the Civil Code, Article 13—the chapter on homicide—paragraph 3, he should be punished at once.

It was then the turn of Senior Advocate Basantaram Bhandari, Charles's solicitor and former chairman of the Supreme Court Chapter of the Nepal Bar Association. He was a renowned expert on the criminal justice system of Nepal. Even though Charles had hired one of the sharpest minds in Nepal to defend him, he couldn't stop himself from passing on advice during the proceedings. Bits of paper, insights and urgent whispers accentuated the case that Bhandari presented. Reportedly, Bhandari didn't seem to mind the unsolicited help; it was rumoured that during his jail terms, Charles had memorized the English translation of the Muluki Ain, Nepal's Civil Code.

Bhandari was succeeded by a few other solicitors, all of whom put forth their points in favour of Charles. The hearing was finished by 1:00 p.m., and it was time for Judge Shrestha to formulate the final verdict. The proceedings had evoked mixed responses from the audience and the press reporters assembled all over the premises. Some believed the case against Charles had little weight; after all, there were no eyewitnesses, no concrete evidence of his presence in Nepal back in 1975. But then, if there were no eyewitnesses to testify against the killer, the killer too had no alibi to prove he hadn't killed.

Shrestha gave his final judgement at 5:00 p.m.

'Sarvoswa sahit janmakaid'

A Nepalese version of life imprisonment of life and soul.

Charles turned red as a beetroot upon hearing the verdict. Sweat flowed down his brow, little droplets pooling around his feet. He walked down the staircase slowly, his face aghast.

'I am going to the toilet,' he said.

'Stop him, he will escape from there!' shouted someone.

*

After my detailed study of the court hearings and the physical and circumstantial evidence admissible under the existing Criminal Act of Nepal, I could find a number of concrete things that incriminated Charles neatly, as clear as day.

1. According to the forensic graphoanalysis, Charles's handwriting resembled that of the guest registration cards at Hotel Malla and Hotel Soaltee. Further, the handwriting of the pseudo Henricus Bintanja matched that of Laurent, pseudo again, in the embarkation and disembarkation cards at Tribhuvan International Airport. Finally, all these handwritings matched the signature in Charles's present passport, the one he had been holding as a French national since 2003.

2. Charles claimed that he was not in Nepal during the time of the crime. However, he could not produce an alibi. There was no evidence at all that he could provide to prove where he had been instead.

3. A copy of the statement that Charles had given at the Lajpat Nagar Court, New Delhi, in 1976, showed that he had confessed to being in Nepal in 1975.

4. All the fingerprint reports matched. The one from New Delhi, the one taken in 1975 by the Kathmandu District Police, and the one taken in 2003 by the Nepal police.

5. The modus operandi of the murders matched. Stabbing repeatedly and burning alive to disguise the identity of the deceased—this was the method of the murder he had been convicted for in India. It was how Connie Jo Bronzich had been killed.

6. In the book, *The Life and Crimes of Charles Sobhraj*, a partial autobiography of Charles penned by Richard Neville and Julie Clarke, there was an in-depth description about Charles's visit to Nepal. It even had a photograph of Connie Jo Bronzich.

Things looked bleak for Charles; the evidence was overwhelming. Yes, the verdict was based primarily on circumstantial evidence, but that was hardly unprecedented for the Nepalese judiciary. On many occasions in the past too, verdicts had been announced based on statements, postmortem reports and fingerprint tests obtained from other countries.

However, I couldn't help but notice several salient points that were in Charles's favour.

1. In 2003, the management of Hotel Soaltee wrote to the Nepal police saying they could not produce original guest registration cards for the investigation.

2. It followed from the previous point that the police had used photocopies of the guest registration cards. But who had arranged photocopies back in 1975? Nepal did not have a photocopy machine back then, and it could almost be said with certainty that the District Police Office did not possess one.

3. The statement and fingerprint reports from the Lajpat Nagar Court of New Delhi did not arrive through a legit, legally admissible channel. It seemed that the American embassy in New Delhi had faxed those papers; the papers had been retrieved by the Delhi branch of Interpol.

4. If Charles did not have an alibi proving that he was *not* in Nepal in 1975, the Nepal police weren't much better. They could not provide evidence that he was.

5. The modus operandi of the murder was considered a crucial piece in the puzzle, the prime circumstantial evidence. However, despite rumours and allegations, there wasn't a proven case of murder against Charles where he had used the stabbing-and-burning-alive method. His alleged murder of Laurent Carriere in Nepal had still not been proved.

6. The book, *The Life and Crimes of Charles Sobhraj*, was less an autobiography, more a novel. Much of the writing was dramatic and could hardly be considered evidence.

7. Charles did not have an alibi. But did that really incriminate him? If someone were to ask even the judge to provide an alibi for his presence at a location thirty years ago, would he be able to do it? It wasn't that straightforward. Plus, Charles Sobhraj, notorious for his cunning and the cocksure manner in which he got things done, could have readily produced an old Goan man to be his alibi. The man could have claimed that Charles had been his tenant for two months, lazing

around in Goa at the time people were being murdered in Nepal. Who would have been able to nullify his claim?

★

Charles challenged the verdict of the Kathmandu District Court in the Appellate Court of Patan. He added Mr Badri Bahadur Karki, a former attorney general of the Government of Nepal, to his fleet of advocates. On 4 August 2005, the Appellate Court announced its final verdict. The joint bench of Judge Krishna Prasad Shrestha and Aatmaram Bhattarai found nothing wrong with the decision of the Kathmandu District Court. Charles's sentence of life imprisonment for the murder of the American citizen, Connie Jo Bronzich, was upheld.

He did not give up easily. He still had the strength to fight, the willingness to be free. This was someone brazen enough to believe that he didn't deserve the sentence he was serving. He wasn't yet the frail man in the hospital who pleaded with me before the surgery, stating that he only wanted to live. Charles filed several petitions to the Supreme Court of Nepal, claiming that his arrest had been illegal, the behaviour towards him, inhuman. It was a violation of international norms. He also filed a case against the prison administration for keeping him in isolation for more than 19 days. Nepalese law, as Charles very well knew, did not allow for any criminal to be detained in solitary confinement for more than 19 days.

In 2008, Charles Sobhraj submitted a plea to the UN Human Rights Committee discussing his 'life sentence following unfair trial'. He sent numerous letters to Mr Ram Baran Yadav and Mr Jhalanath Khanal, who were the president and the prime minister of Nepal, respectively, at that time. His French advocate— Isabelle Coutant Peyre—handled all his correspondence for him.

The international media picked up all of this, reporting on the developments, but staying non-committal.

Everything turned out to be futile. Everyone turned a deaf ear to the brutal murderer who was finally lying in the bed he had made for himself.

✷

After the verdict had been passed and Charles's pleas had gone unheard, the Government of Nepal received a letter from John B. Calaborn, the father of Connie Jo Bronzich. He dispatched a letter through the embassy of the USA in Nepal, commending the Nepalese authorities for convicting the murderer of his daughter, after almost three decades.

> Mrs Calaborn and I would like to express our deepest gratitude to the Nepalese authorities for their dedication and relentless pursuit of justice for the man responsible for the murder of our daughter. We realize that the successful apprehension and conviction of Charles Sobhraj required many hours of investigation and a great degree of proficiency on the part of those who were involved.
>
> We would like to express our deep appreciation for all those involved in the case, especially ex-Inspector Bishwa Lal Shrestha, DSP Ganesh KC, Attorney Suryanath Prakash Adhikary and Judge Bishwombhar Prasad Shrestha.

14

THE QUEST FOR
THE ANSWER CONTINUES

In 2003, there were nearly 190 countries in the world. Charles Sobhraj was free and living a happy life in France. Only one country in the world had active cases of murder against him—Nepal. And yet it was Nepal that Charles decided to visit, again. Why on earth did he come to Nepal, only to find himself behind bars?

My question remained unanswered. The many conversations I had had with Charles hadn't answered the question that disturbed and rattled me. Ganesh K.C., the police officer who had caught Charles in Nepal, had boasted to the media, 'He is kept under special security arrangements in prison. He may have escaped from Tihar in India, but he cannot elude us. Charles Sobhraj made a huge mistake in returning to Nepal.'

Whenever I read that statement or thought about it, the question in my head only became bigger. It was a puzzle I had to solve at any cost.

★

'So, Alain, tell me the motive behind your last visit to Nepal.'
I was sitting on a cosy chair in my dream, facing one of the
most notorious killers the world has known.

'This is my first and only visit here,' he answered calmly.
He could probably repeat this sentence in his sleep; he had
said it so often.

'Okay! Tell me the reason behind your first visit then. We
both know it was not for the pashmina or the mineral water.'
The spot boy jiggled with the lights noisily; he was probably
trying to make me look less dark and rugged when compared
to our fair-skinned, handsome guest.

'I was here for two different things. One, I wanted to
organize an undercover business meeting of some guys from
the Taliban with a Chinese heroin producer in the Golden Triads.
And second one was a meeting with top brass from India.'

'Chinese?'

'Well, he is a Burmese citizen of Chinese descent. We
became friends when I was in Thailand. I lost touch with him
when I left Bangkok, but somehow managed to track him down.'

'Do you have close ties with the Taliban?'

'Do you know Masood?'

'You mean the Islamist terrorist who was with you in Tihar?'

'Yes. He introduced me to all the Taliban leaders. That's
actually why I visited Afghanistan several times.'

I winced. I had seen some photographs of him in
Afghanistan. He had supposedly been there for a humanitarian
mission. Humanitarian, my foot!

'I had good relations with the Taliban and the al-Qaeda.

You know, I even had a nuclear deal with Saddam Hussein.' His revelations got more chilling by the minute. They also started sounding ludicrous.

'What?'

'Yes. I had a business contract to supply red mercury to Iraq and had already made a deal with a Russian group. But then, 2003 happened.' For the life of me, I could not decipher if he referred to the 2003 attack on Iraq by the USA or his 2003 arrest in Nepal. Probably both? But in either case, had the incidents of 2003 unfolded differently, he would have probably been supplying red mercury to Saddam Hussein. The latter would have probably used it in a nuclear missile smuggled from the Russian military. I didn't want to imagine what might have happened next.

Our conversation was becoming too long for a half-an-hour television programme. Even with tight editing, it would easily make for two episodes. But I didn't mind. The TRPs were likely to be excellent, and the management could even push it to three episodes. My guest was in a particularly talkative mood, and I was not foolish to stop him.

He went on. 'One day in early September, I was driving to Marseille when I got a call from Reik. He said it was an emergency. The man was frantically screaming about the 9/11 attack. You know, the al-Qaeda had done exactly what I had warned the CIA about.'

I stared at the serial killer sitting in front of me, occasionally sipping from his cup of coffee. This murderer, this con man, claimed to know about the 9/11 before it happened. He had supposedly known in advance about that unprecedented attack on the World Trade Center, one of the most gruesome events witnessed by the world.

'America vowed to finish off the terrorists, of course. You know, America had always had good relations with the Taliban. It was well known that the CIA had sponsored the Mujahideen to fight against Russian invasion in Afghanistan. Later, a fraction of those who had been in the Mujahideen converted to Taliban. And Taliban had good ties with the al-Qaeda, the numero uno foe of the USA.'

He paused for breath before continuing to share his insights on the role of the USA in the formation of the Taliban.

'What happened then?'

'As the USA helped them grow, they always had infiltration from the al-Qaeda and the Taliban. In fact, now, they had their sources in the ISIS. But after the 9/11 attack, all the strings between the CIA and the al-Qaeda were broken. It was then that they contacted me. They knew I wanted to help every country I could when it came to fighting against terrorism. I hate how terrorists kill innocent people. I hate killing people.'

Of course, you hate killing people, I thought. *It pains you and makes you cry whenever you strangle and stab people, burning them alive and walking away amidst their harrowing screams.* 'So, how did you help now?' I somehow forced myself to stick to the questions in the script.

'After the US strike on Afghanistan, the al-Qaeda and the Taliban stopped using electronic devices for communication. The US intelligence agencies were finding it difficult to trace their moves. As the CIA already knew about my good relations with the top dogs in the Taliban, they contacted me immediately to strike a deal. They wanted me to gain the faith of the Taliban, infiltrate into their systems and share any information I could gather with the USA.'

'Then what was your plan?' I cursed myself for not being

well-informed about Islamic jihadists. But truth be told, I had not expected my interview with a French serial killer to take this turn. I wondered if my nervousness was palpable on the screen. My sweat sure was, and I signalled a crew member to lower the temperature settings of the air conditioner.

'Well, I found that the best trap was opium. Afghanistan was the leading producer of opium, and almost the entire trade was governed by the Taliban. They had been struggling for the last few years because the CIA had got wind of the opium trade and started surveillance on their route. If they found someone who could help them with this, someone who could rev up the trade again, it would be a great foundation for a relationship. I shared my plan with the CIA.'

'Then?' I sounded dumb even to myself, asking monosyllabic questions for quite a long time now.

'Then, well, they accepted my plan and funded my tours. My goal was to provide an excellent business deal to the Taliban, something they couldn't refuse. I mean, imagine their angst—the biggest producers of opium, controlling nearly 90 per cent of the world trade, but stuck without a place to sell!'

I let him continue.

'It took me almost two years to convince the Taliban for a long-term deal. I was sure that a factory in Burma or Thailand would be the right choice; I knew these things. But thirty years is a rather long time; I had lost contact.'

I suspected he was now talking about the Golden Triads. Old movies I had seen flashed in front of my eyes. There was the Hindi movie, *Drishyam*, where the protagonist, Vijay Salgaonkar, was a movie freak and watched every film he could find. His exposure to all these films—a good number of them thrillers and crime movies—helped him fool the police when he was trying to save his wife and daughter from a murder charge. Then there was the Hollywood movie, *The Usual Suspects,* where a character—Dean Keaton—would cook up different stories from the noticeboards he had seen at police stations. It wasn't all that difficult to fool people, not even the police, especially when you have the gift of the gab, the right information, and the courage to implement this information.

Here, in my TV show, I was witness to a live demonstration of this hoodwinking. I couldn't believe a word of what he was saying. He was an avid reader with a keen interest in law, and, I presumed, also kept himself aware of all the happenings around the world. He was smartly implanting himself in many of these events, trying to pull off a big-time conspiracy theory.

'I went hunting for them,' Alain went on, evidently enjoying the tale. 'It wasn't easy. Again, it took me nearly two years to contact them and finalize a deal for the profitable supply of raw material for heroin.'

I was swiftly losing interest in this heroin talk, obviously fabricated. 'Okay, let's talk about your second meeting. What was that Indian top brass about?'

'Oh, it was a meeting with the IB,' he said as casually as if he was meeting friends for brunch.

'You mean the Intelligence Bureau of India? What for?'

'I helped them from time by time. It was me who facilitated the return of that hijacked Indian Airlines plane from Kandahar.'

The reveals were now mounting one on top of the other. It was happening so swiftly that I felt as if Alain was the host and I was merely a spot boy whose sole responsibility was to ensure the air conditioner operated at full blast.

'Can you imagine,' Alain continued with a smug look, 'Advani escaped an assassination due to my tip?'

I gulped down another glass of water, perhaps my third since the interview had started. 'Would you care to explain that?'

'With pleasure. So, I happened to get the information that two large-scale attacks were being planned in New Delhi. The IB was able to uncover one of them with my help—the attack targeting Lal Krishna Advani, the home minister at the time. They increased his security, and the attackers could not complete their mission. The other attack went undiscovered—they blew up the Parliament.'

'Ah, so you could at least save Advani.' I wondered if my sarcasm could be heard over the scratchiness of my throat. I drank some more water, attempting to clear my voice.

'His daughter and mine are good friends. I love him very much; he's a true Indian.' Alain never missed a chance to establish his relationships with people in power. Why, hadn't I too been established as a relative not long ago?

'So, did the Advani incident cement your ties with the IB?'

'Oh yes. After that, I had a great rapport with the IB. I used to give them information related to terrorist activities in India. And this time, we were planning to discuss Kashmir and Lashkar-e-Taiba. IB was happy to fund Taliban in Afghanistan only to create instability in the western border of Pakistan. It was to be a type of revenge, you know?'

'No, I don't know,' I snapped. 'I am not a journalist privileged enough to know about such undercover international politics.'

'Fair enough,' he nodded. 'Anyway, it was a win-win situation for me. I was hired by different groups to perform a similar kind of business. Good money too!'

'Okay,' I breathed deeply, preparing to ask him the question I had been leading up to. 'But why did you choose Kathmandu? Didn't you know that you had two murder investigations awaiting you in the Nepalese capital?'

'They had no case against me! I had never been here. There were no witnesses, no proof. You know, I got a tourist visa from the Nepalese consulate in Paris. If they had had anything against me, wouldn't they have denied me entry?'

Wait, this did not sound right. He could not have been so foolish! 'So, Nepal was *your* decision?' I asked, open-mouthed.

'They gave me five options: Colombo, Kathmandu, Dubai, Bangkok and Karachi. Bangkok was impossible. The Chinese guys rejected Dubai and Karachi; Pakistan and the Emirates are not safe for drug dealers. It had to be either Colombo or Kathmandu.'

'What was wrong with Bangkok? They have nothing against you anymore.'

'They don't, of course, but I still had enemies lurking in the shadows. That bloody Knippenberg, for example, was sure to be hovering under an alias, waiting for a chance to kill me.'

'So, you finalized Kathmandu?'

'Yes, mainly because China had good ties with Mahindra Rajapaksa, who was the Sri Lankan president. The IB decided that Kathmandu would be safer. Since I knew every nook and corner here, it would be safer still.'

'But you said you had never visited Kathmandu before!' Aha, finally there was a trap he had fallen into headlong.

He didn't respond; I persevered. 'Did you get that kind of acquaintance with Kathmandu from Google Maps? Those maps are good, I have heard.'

He maintained his silence. After a moment or two, he lifted his right hand and gestured for me to end the interview. It would be awfully abrupt to end it on that note, but what did he care?

I remembered something I overheard while Shakuntala Didi

was whispering to his doctor a while back. 'He is not afraid of Knippenberg; he is afraid of the CIA. It is the CIA that ditched him.'

*

Charles was quite the storyteller, even in my dreams which were frequent and invariably on the same lines. He was so used to running around, looting and killing people, planning one jailbreak after the other, that the slow prison life bored him to death. Perhaps Charles Sobhraj intended to write a book about his fantasies in jail. If he ever did write one, I would gladly recommend the perfect title:

The Earth Revolves Around ME!

15

CAUGHT OR TRAPPED?

'Charles, I need to know one more thing about your trial in Nepal.'

'It's baseless,' he responded, even before I could complete the question. 'I was sentenced without any evidence whatsoever.'

'Yes, about that—who do you think was behind it all? The Nepal police? Or the Government of Nepal?'

'No, it was Knippenberg. And his money. Did you know the then inspector Bishwa Lal was expelled from the police because he had been caught taking bribes?' Charles looked disgusted. 'Trust me, I know what money can do.'

'It's the CIA, Bhanja,' whispered Shakuntala in my head again, 'He is just afraid to spell it out loud.'

I thought of Herman Knippenberg, a Dutch diplomat previously based in Bangkok, who had been the one to put the Thai police on Sobhraj's trail. He had started investigating the case independently after the murder of the Dutch couple in Thailand. His evidence had been incriminating—documents belonging to the deceased, drugs used to poison people, etc. It was curious how an individual, unrelated to the police or the murder victims, had unearthed so much evidence. If Knippenberg had done it once, what was to say he couldn't have done it all over again? Perhaps he was the one to put the Nepal police on Charles's trail in 1975. Perhaps he was the secret enemy Charles had never intended to make, the enemy who proved to be his undoing.

✶

'Let the skeletons remain buried in the closet,' Subry said to me over the phone that morning, his voice serious for once. 'You are worrying far too much about that criminal.'

I knew I was. But I didn't know how to stop. Charles's trial at the Kathmandu District Court had been long over; he had already served almost 15 years of imprisonment. Even after all this time, I couldn't stop wondering about the discrepancies in the court documents that Shakuntala had shared with me. Charles had been sentenced to life imprisonment without eyewitnesses, without tangible evidence. And yet, the courts of Nepal had been known to release convicts merely on the basis of an eyewitness account. 'Your honour, the killer was wearing a red shirt,' an eyewitness could say, 'And this man was wearing pink. He couldn't have killed.' And bingo! That might have been enough.

The newspapers were flooded with reports of arrests at the India-Nepal border. Terrorists, gangsters, murderers—they all seemingly lurked at the border, hatching evil plans.

August 2013. Yasin Bhatkal, the founder leader of

Mujahideen, was arrested on the India-Nepal border.

May 2017. Naseer Ahmed, a Hizbul Mujahideen terrorist, was arrested by the Indo-Nepal border guarding force. He had been illegally entering India to carry out a terrorist mission.

January 2018. Abdul Subhan Qureshi, a dangerous terrorist India had been trying to track down for years, was arrested at the India-Nepal border.

February 2018. Mukhiya Gurung, a murderer who had killed a man in Kathmandu 18 years ago and had been on the run ever since, was arrested in Jaipur, India. Magically, the next day, the Nepal police also arrested him from Mahendranagar, a bordering town in western Nepal.

Aziz Khan, an alleged Indian Mujahideen terrorist linked to the serial blasts in Uttar Pradesh, India, was arrested from the India-Nepal border.

Manoj Pun, a gangster and suspect in the murders of several businessmen in Nepal, was arrested from the India-Nepal border. He tried to escape even as the police were bringing him to the station. The man was killed in an encounter.

Nepal and India had never signed an extradition treaty. However, it was a common practice for both the countries to exchange criminals, depending on the country where they committed their crimes. The official versions were always arrested at some Indo-Nepal border. And yet, nothing of that sort had happened with Charles Sobhraj. On 4 August 1976, the Crime Investigation Cell of Nepal police had to write an official letter to the Home Ministry of India, asking for the extradition of Charles Sobhraj. After his term at the Tihar Jail was complete, India had nowhere to deport the stateless man. They bargained with the French government and managed to secure a French nationality for Charles. Why didn't India hand him over to Nepal instead, transferring his custody to the Nepal police at Mahendranagar? Why did his jail term in Nepal not begin seamlessly from where it had ended in India?

*

'I remember the day as if it was yesterday. It was a foggy and quiet morning. I was playing near the airport. Back in 1975, there were only fields in that area. I was running up the green fields, when suddenly, I saw policemen in front of me. They were all gathered around a dead body—the naked, burned corpse of a young white woman. The body was completely charred, except the head. It was perhaps the most horrifying moment of my life.'

A 12-year-old boy had seen Connie Jo Bronzich's burnt body near the Manahara River. It had haunted him at night, the sight of that burnt, lifeless body lying half-hidden in the morning fog. The boy was now a police officer. Coincidentally, it was he who had arrested one of the most sought-after serial killers of all times, the murderer of the white woman from all those years ago.

Really, when it came to Charles, I was stupefied by the number of coincidences that sprung up from nowhere. Unfortunately for him, many of these incidents did not turn out to be favourable.

On 4 August 1976, a new forensic handwriting analysis report came out. 'The signatures on the embarkation and disembarkation cards at the Tribhuvan International Airport resemble those on the guest registration cards of Hotel Soaltee and Hotel Malla. However, it cannot be conclusively said that they belong to the same person.' Contrast this with the report that came out on the 7 October 2003. It was a forensic graphoanalysis report prepared by the Nepal police. The report claimed that the signatures on the guest registration cards of both the hotels matched the signature on Charles Sobhraj's French passport. 'There are common writing characteristics between the signatures that suggest the probability of common authorship.' Even though this report was more strongly worded than the previous one, it still suggested a probability, not a confirmation. But this *probability* had seemingly helped to build a *strong* case against someone who was widely believed to be a monster. It didn't take much to give a dog a bad name and then hang him, after all.

The Nepal police promptly produced photocopies of the guest registration cards—card number 6449 of Hotel Soaltee and card number 0119 of Hotel Malla. The provider of these photocopies remains mysterious. But such was the power of these photocopied cards that they too contributed to the already terrible charges against Charles, never mind how photocopied evidence had never been considered valid by the Nepalese judiciary system before.

K	M	P	S	1	2	3	F
15-w	2	5	A	1	9	X	8
		17	R	1	9		4

A scientific tabulation of fingerprints obtained from Charles Sobhraj

The book, *The Life and Crimes of Charles Sobhraj*, another 'major' evidence in the case against Charles also presented a puzzling situation. In 1975, Mr Chandrabir Rai, then Superintendent of Police, had summoned Henricus Bintanja to his office regarding the murder of Connie Jo Bronzich. According to the book, he had only asked the Dutchman a few questions, rather impressed by his scholarly personality. Rai had been more suspicious of Laurent Carriere, considering him the likeliest to have committed the murder. Rai had interrogated several people even remotely connected to the case, including the owner of the Oriental Lodge where Connie had been staying, and her friends, Sally, Luke and Katy.

In 2003, the Nepal police had reproduced fingerprints of Henricus Bintanja as taken in 1975 by Rai . Did the Nepal police regularly take fingerprints of everyone they questioned? It sure didn't seem conventional. Why hadn't Rai taken the fingerprints of the people Connie had been staying with or the owner of the lodge? Surely, they would have been bigger suspects than the outsider, Henricus?

On 5 January 1977, the Bhaktapur District Court had announced its verdict on the murder of Laurent Carriere. 'His murder is confirmed. However, there is no information about the convict or the motive. If and when the public prosecutor gathers any evidence or insight, the case will be reopened.'

It had never been reopened. Not even after Charles was arrested for murdering Connie, a case so intimately entwined with the murder of Laurent. The Nepalese Criminal Act, the Civil Code, stated that if a person had committed different crimes in different places, all the cases should be merged in one court. But neither the public prosecutor nor the Bhaktapur District Court had bothered with Laurent again.

There were too many wrinkles, too many unanswered questions in the events that had led up to Charles's arrest in Nepal. The judiciary and the police both seemed oblivious to these glaring loopholes, not caring tuppence about a man called Charles Sobhraj, then serving a jail term in Golghar in Central Jail, Nepal. The Nepal Civil Code allowed a term-waiver for well-behaved prisoners who had completed half their sentence and were over 70 years of age. The waiver could be activated for about 23 types of crimes, including murder. And so the serpent remained in Nepal prison, not attempting to escape, no one interested in scrambling through the cobwebs that had settled on his decades-old trial in court.

I wondered if the whole thing had been a trap for Sobhraj. A snake trap for a venomous snake that could bite more people if not caught. If it had indeed been a trap, who had planted it? What did the Nepalese government, judiciary or police stand to gain from his arrest?

★

I could not figure it out. Who was to blame, who was blameless? If the discrepancies in the legal proceedings bugged me, Charles too had a history of fishy, extremely odd deeds.

After his release from Tihar jail, he had gone to Paris. However, I had seen dozens of pictures on the Internet and documentaries that showed Charles in Afghanistan. What was he doing there? Was he really doing some undercover business with the Taliban and Chinese drug dealers?

His visit to Nepal, of course, remained the most curious question of all. Every Nepalese man and woman knows about a Frenchman named Charles Sobhraj, a serial killer who had probably committed the murders along the hippie trail in Nepal. But notwithstanding that, the Nepalese embassy in Paris had issued a tourist visa to him.

How did he enter unnoticed through the immigration checkpoint at Tribhuvan International Airport in Kathmandu?

Who tipped the editor of *The Himalayan Times* about Charles's presence in Nepal?

Why didn't Charles fly back to Paris after his photo was published, garnering much national interest and attention?

Was his claimed business of pashmina and mineral water worth the risk of arrest or did he let overconfidence become his undoing again?

Had a powerful authority—yes, the CIA—assured him that nothing would happen?

I couldn't help thinking that there was some truth, albeit slim, in his claims of being deployed in Nepal on an undercover mission. Perhaps he had indeed served the CIA? But now that his role was over or possibly because someone suspected danger, it was time for him to be put down.

What could be a better way of decimating someone than securing for them a sentence of life imprisonment? After you have broken away from jail as many times as Charles had, and attained the notoriety he enjoyed, there's only so much freedom your final prison will give you.

✳

It was twilight in the Kathmandu valley. We were at the foothills of the Shivapuri, the 2000-metre hillock we planned to ascend in preparation for our Thorang-La trek. Around us, the valley was fully illuminated, little lights on in all the cottages and buildings. I marvelled at the feat as I sipped my beer; back in the city, we had been suffering from 18 hours of load-shedding every day.

We were staying with Saheeb—an ex-police officer and Comrade's college mate—in his newly built bungalow. This was the first time I was meeting Saheeb, but I felt as if I had known him longer. His sense of humour and vast knowledge of the medical field soon made us good friends.

'Kulman has done a marvellous job,' said Saheeb, looking

around the valley. 'Before he became the director at the electricity authority, we'd always have to live in the darkness of bribery.'

A plump lady, supposedly his wife, appeared in the doorway and walked towards us with a tray. 'Meet Raamesh Koirala,' said Saheeb, 'He's a doctor at Gangalal.'

'Namaste, Bhauju,'[7] I greeted her as she started spreading snacks on the table. She smiled back at me, showing not the faintest hint of recognition of either my face or my name.

'You know Charles Sobhraj?' Saheeb went on. 'It was he who operated on his heart.'

And voila! She paused midway, a few crumbs of chiura[8] spilling onto the table. Even after she had returned to the house, leaving us drinking in the garden, I thought I saw her once, silently parting the curtains to stare at the surgeon who had saved a murderer's life.

Saheeb's manner of introducing me had changed the tone of the evening. We stopped talking about Kulman and his honest endeavour to bring electricity to the villages of Nepal. Saheeb's son and his ongoing studies at the All India Institute of Medical Sciences, New Delhi, also got relegated to the back-burner. My high-profile patient and his tales were far spicier than the chiura Saheeb's wife had brought for us on a tray.

This was a good opportunity to get some perspective on the case. A senior police officer could surely quell some of my doubts. 'Why was Charles sentenced—and that too such a harsh sentence—without concrete evidence? What do you think?'

He took some time before asking me a counter question,

---

[7] Nepali for sister-in-law
[8] A popular snack made of flattened rice

'Do you know about the Robinson case, doctor saab?'

I sure did. The Robinson case had occured about four months before Charles's final verdict came out. I had never seen judges at the receiving end of so much public wrath before. In April 2004, a bench of two judges at the Supreme Court gave a clean chit to Gordon William Robinson, an alleged British drug trafficker, challenging the judgement previously delivered by a lower court. Robinson had been arrested in 2001 at Tribhuvan International Airport; he had been carrying more than two kilograms of brown sugar on his person. A special court had sentenced him to imprisonment of 17 years. However, a curious thing happened at the Supreme Court—the police statement was found questionable. Had the heroin been confiscated from his left shoes or right? How could Robinson possibly be guilty if the police muddled up *such* an important detail? A free man, he left Nepal faster than anyone could say Jack Robinson. The media was aghast. Almost regularly, there were scathing cover stories about alleged bribery in the case. Probes were ordered against the judges. While one of them abruptly resigned, the other claimed to be innocent until proved otherwise.

'The social boycott, media bashing, and allegations of corruption ruined the lives of those two judges,' said Saheeb. 'I have a strong feeling the judge overseeing Charles's case did not want a repeat telecast of those events. The Robinson case was fresh in public memory; it was just unfortunate timing. Otherwise, I am sure you could find Judge Shrestha in North Carolina today, singing lullabies to Charles's granddaughter.'

It made sense. If I, a surgeon, had suffered so much mental turmoil before treating Charles, even though I was professionally required to do it, what must the judge have experienced? Who would want to release a man everyone believed to be a beast?

'What about his petition in the Supreme Court?'

'It won't get a date until his life sentence is over, mark my words. He is going to die here in prison.'

A few days ago, the doctor-in-charge of the Central Jail had called me to check on Charles. He had been concerned for his health, as usual, asking me pointed questions about his recovery. And he was also as sure as Saheeb that he would face another charge as soon as the recent one finished. A criminal case lay neatly prepared for him at the Bhaktapur District Court—the murder of Laurent Carriere.

Saheeb's words sounded ominous to me. *He is going to die here in prison.* I felt sure that even if Charles was to get magically pardoned for the murders, he would somehow be found with 200 grams of brown sugar. He would promptly be arrested again, right from the courtyard of the Central Jail, this time for illegal possession of drugs.

'*He would never leave Nepal alive.*'

16

A CONVICT AGAIN

'When do you want to be discharged?' I asked Charles Sobhraj one morning, 'You are fine and ready to go.'

It had been about a week since his surgery, and he had recovered faster than anyone would have speculated. He sat up in his bed, reading the newspaper. The recent decision of the traffic police in Nepal was the biggest news of the day; apparently, they had withdrawn the penalty on pedestrians who didn't cross the roads at zebra crossings. People were back to strolling idly, treating the roads like public gardens, no longer afraid of being fined. The government had announced a compensation for the family of the girl who had been hit by a microbus. The 'martyr' would always be remembered, said the government, and her family would receive one million rupees as compensation.

Charles kept the newspaper aside and looked up at me. 'Doctor, I want complete recovery. I want to gain my strength before I get back. You know the conditions there are abysmal.'

I couldn't deny he was right. The doctor-in-charge of the Central Jail had also insisted that Charles make a complete recovery before returning to prison. He was afraid of bacterial endocarditis—an infection that can be fatal for patients who have recently undergone a surgery. The French embassy had written to the hospital too, asking us to detain Charles until he was, pretty much, in the pink of health.

But it was easier said than done.

'What do you mean by full recovery?' I asked Charles, aware that my question was rather redundant. 'You had a heart surgery, and getting fully up on your feet may take two to three months.' Keeping him at Gangalal for three months was a proposition laden with risk. Already, his feet had started fitting properly inside his torn Chinese shoes. His urinary incontinence had vanished. If he escaped from the hospital, a sniffing dog would be unable to sniff out leaking urine.

'I will arrange for those bed-tables,' suggested Charles, as if that was the prime obstacle lying between him and a prolonged hospital stay. 'If you want, I can also give an interview about your hospital and mention that it has excellent services. You will get good business. People from all around the world will start coming to Nepal for treatment.'

I let myself imagine for a moment the picture that Charles was painting. Medical tourism was the last thing Nepal could advertise, considering it was unable to provide even basic medical services to its countrymen. Dreaming of foreigners coming here for treatment was absurd. It only became asinine when I pictured Charles Sobhraj—a murderer—as the ambassador of this lofty dream.

I was about to chastise him for trying to sell me the moon

when my phone rang. It was Ojaswi, Subry's wife. 'Dai, where are you?' She sounded rather panic-stricken.

'What happened, Oju?'

'Subry had an accident. He has cut his little finger. Here, please talk to him.'

Subry's voice came through the phone, alarmed and slightly intoxicated. 'I am near Gangalal. I slipped on the mud at the dratted construction site.'

'Whom should I blame? Your flip-flops, the monsoon or beer?'

'Don't make jokes, Dai. It is bleeding heavily.'

'Don't worry, go directly to the ICU. I will ask Nirmal to look at your wound and sew it. I need to go to my sister's, but if there's anything serious, he will call me.'

At my sister's house that evening, my brother-in-law had quite a treat ready—dried meat of deer and beer in large glasses. Deer meat was a delicacy in Nepal, available in almost every restaurant. The two of us were relishing the meat, sumptuously prepared by my sister, when Subry called.

'I am doing fine now, Dai,' he announced cheerily, 'Nirmal stitched the cut nice and proper.'

'That's great.' I was pleased to hear his cheerful voice; Subry was usually happy and content, and I hated seeing him in any other way. On an impulse, I decided to give him a treat.

'Subry, would you like to visit Charles?'

'Oh, definitely!' he answered in a trice, unthinking and excited.

'Right. Nirmal will take you up to him.'

★

Three weeks had passed since Charles Sobhraj's surgery—three times longer than the average hospital stay after a conventional heart valve surgery. 'Complete' recovery or not, his discharge couldn't possibly be delayed any longer. I was almost surprised it had been that long—where had the time passed?

'You are ready to be discharged,' I told Charles, firmly this time. 'Please arrange accordingly.'

'Doctor! Reik is coming next week.' He sidestepped me neatly, focusing instead on his British journalist friend. Even though Charles had plagued me day after day, asking if Reik had called, he never had.

'Why is he coming?' I asked cautiously.

'He is coming to help free me from this injustice. He is bringing two lawyers with him too.'

'Really? I thought lawyers without local registration are not allowed to take part in Supreme Court hearings.'

'Well, who's to stop them from studying my case and prodding the local lawyers along?'

I cleared my throat in a rather feeble attempt to get back to the subject. 'You will need to come to the hospital once every two weeks for a month. After discharge, make sure not to eat any food that interacts with your blood-thinning medicine, you know, like that liver pickle from your friends at the French embassy.'

He ignored my statement yet again, choosing instead to sit up straighter and talk excitedly about something else altogether. 'Doctor, I am planning to write a book about myself. I will put in a chapter about my illness and discuss how you helped treat me. Is that okay with you?' He continued before I had a chance to respond. 'I mean, you will become famous! People from all over the world will come to you.'

What a people-pleaser he was, forever weaving tales, glorifying other people. Bribing his way out of jail. Keeping himself out of Golghar, the isolation cell, with sweet talk. I had a strong urge to tell him something I too had been planning for a while. 'Likewise, I, too, may write a book about you. But I would need written consent. What do you think?'

'Anything you want, doctor. Bring a consent paper tomorrow. I will sign it.'

I couldn't believe that he had agreed so readily. But then, he had always enjoyed the limelight; the umpteenth book or film could never hurt. That evening, I typed out a consent form seeking his permission to allow me to reveal his medical condition as well as the case against him in the Supreme Court of Nepal.

'I will get it checked by my lawyers,' he said, skimming through the papers I handed to him the next morning.

Neither of us talked about the discharge again. But both of us knew it was imminent, and nothing could be done to postpone it any longer.

30 June 2017, 6:30 p.m.

Kathmandu was half-lit with artificial lights, the other half was still waiting to reduce their electricity bills by a few paisa, if not more, thanks to the 'end of decades-long load-shedding'. Charles Sobhraj's discharge papers, laboratory reports and required drugs were ready. I had advised him to continue Warfarin, Spironolactone, Atorvastatin, Metoprolol and Lasix. The paperwork in the accounts department was in the clear. Everyone was ready for the discharge. It was late evening but a lot of the staff, including me, had stayed back.

We had decided that evening time would be best for Charles's discharge as there was likely to be a smaller crowd in the lobby. A police van arrived at the portico of the hospital building. Even though I had stayed back, I didn't particularly want a goodbye scene with Charles. So, I remained in my cabin and presently parted the curtains on the window to peer out. An elderly man was being escorted by five policemen, all of them guarding him closely and leaving no space for a potential escape. The van drove away in the swiftly darkening evening, blowing up some dust on the portico.

I knew Charles would be back for outpatient check-ups and I would be the one to conduct them. But somehow, that day, he ceased being my patient. He stopped being someone admitted to a hospital, recovering from surgery. Once more, he was a convict, hated by millions of people. It felt like a reverse metamorphosis—a butterfly, free and pure, going back to a cocoon, only to be transformed into a hideous caterpillar.

Fortunately, there was a cricket match that night, and it helped channel my thoughts away from Charles and his impending doom. Dhoni emerged as the top scorer, securing 78 runs and leading India to victory. He was finally inching closer to 10,000 runs.

*

In my childhood, I learnt that Nepal went into a state of trance twice every year. The first was during Durga Puja when grand idols of Goddess Durga were prepared from clay and painted in vibrant colours, the second during Saraswati Puja. Pandals or temporary tent-temples would be erected and decorated, prizes would be given out to the best-decorated pandal in every region. The day the puja would end, the idols would be put on the back of a truck and taken for immersion to the Mechi River. Devotees would follow the trucks, singing and dancing, chanting 'Jai Ho!' The procession would return late in the evening, everyone's faces curiously bittersweet. It was a joyous occasion, symbolic of the victory of good over evil, of happy endings and new beginnings. And yet, it was the most heartbreaking thing ever. On the day of Charles's discharge, I felt similar emotions well up inside me.

I was happy to see the old, septuagenarian man walking out from my hospital after a successful surgery. I remembered how frail he had looked all those weeks ago, barely able to move. And look at him now! But I also felt sorry—and a little guilty—for prolonging the life of a serial killer. What had I done?

Sorry, Connie Jo Bronzich!

Sorry, Laurent Carriere!

Sorry! I wanted to cry out loud, to everyone who had lost their lives at the hands of this evil, deceptive man.

But I don't think any of them heard me.

17

AFTERMATH

'Next Sunday is my trial. By next month, I will be in France.' If they wanted a theme song for Charles's outpatient visits, it should have been this. It was his perpetual refrain during every visit to update me on his 'upcoming trials' and impending release from jail. I usually paid little attention. The workload at the hospital was a lot, and I had several patients to examine every day. A lot was going on in Nepal too, particularly interesting of which was the completion of the local-level elections. Since Subry took an immense interest in politics, he would regale us with stories about Bharatpur's new mayor who, by the by, had allegedly won only because her supporters had torn some ballot papers.

In those days, I was also preparing very seriously for our upcoming trek. Every weekend, the Thorang-La aspirants would go hiking to the nearby hills in preparation for the big, final trek. Sudeep was helping us tremendously, offering his trekking lessons free of cost.

Do you have three-tier clothing?

Are your T-shirts breathable?

Do you know how to hold the trekking pole?

No, it is *not* 'just a walking stick'!

After the exhaustive trekking lessons by Sudeep, I was somewhat surprised with what happened during one of our weekend hikes. We were hiking to Nagarjun in the northwest of the Kathmandu valley, 1970 metres above the sea level. It seemed easy enough, especially for aspirants aiming to trek to 5416 metres soon. But at about 1900 metres, quite a long way from the top, we had to abandon the plan. Sudeep was having serious trouble breathing. It turned out, even though he knew a lot about high-altitude trekking, theory didn't always pan out well in practice.

One afternoon, I was in my cabin, examining Chheten, a patient and friend I sometimes chatted with about my trekking trips. He lived up in the hills and often gave me good advice on the places with the best views.

Charles Sobhraj was waiting in the lobby. He visited the hospital far more often than we had advised him to. The same bunch of policemen came along with him each time. I was getting sick of seeing policemen in the lobby every week; it always took me by surprise.

'Chheten Dai,' I ignored Charles and said to my patient, 'What do you suggest? Ghyaru or Manang?'

'Go to Ghyaru. It is one of the most beautiful places up there.' Chheten volunteered to be our host for one day and also offered to book hotels for us along the trail.

'Are my blood reports in yet, doctor?' Charles called out from his seat. He could never be patient when someone preceded him in importance. On every visit, he *had* to be the first one. Even if 80 odd patients sat awaiting their turn, I had to spend about 30 minutes answering his questions first. Some of the things he'd chat about were inane.

I couldn't bring myself to indulge him this time and examined his reports only after Chheten had left. 'You need to take three milligrams of Warfarin instead of two. Everything else seems okay.'

He nodded and handed over a sheaf of papers to me, beaming from end to end. 'It's the consent you wanted. Everything looks okay here too. Get someone to type it out, and I will sign it on my next visit.'

'Thanks,' I glanced at the papers quickly and put them in the drawer. It was quite a lot of writing—his lawyers were thorough—and there were two different kinds of ink too. Lately, it seemed, I was getting a lot of reading material. Shakuntala had visited a few days ago and had handed over another sheaf of papers.

'These are papers from his court hearings, his petition to the UN Human Rights Committee, and a letter to the president of Nepal. If you need anything else, you only have to let me know.'

Those papers lay in the drawer too, some of them getting mixed up with my consent. My consent for writing about the criminal whose period of life imprisonment I had helped prolong.

*

Between July and September that year, my days alternated between attending to Charles and my other patients in the outpatient cabin and taking trekking lessons from Comrade.

Now that Sudeep had abandoned the group, Comrade had taken his place. He purchased a few Motorola walkie-talkies, choosing Motorola mainly because the controversy surrounding NCell had soured his heart. 'We will use this hi-tech mode of communication for the upcoming trek.' He announced one weekend, as we stood at the foothills of the Shivapuri, 2732 metres. 'I have got them registered with the Department of Communication and the police department in Nepal. Do you think I should also carry a satellite phone?' He dismissed that idea only after we guffawed for fifteen minutes.

Trekking was extremely pleasurable just then, the weather bright and the views vivid. Moreover, our trekking trails were safe from danger and mental turmoil, unlike the corridors of the hospital or the territory of my dreams, both of which sometimes worked me up in a sweat. For that matter, the hippie trail was now safe too, devoid of the beast that had haunted it for many years. The German ambassador Matthias Meyer had finally reached home; it had taken him one and a half months to cross the hippie trail in his white Mitsubishi and reach Hanover in Germany.

July and September—or Shrawan and Bhadra according to the Hindu solar calendar—were also the months of fasting in Nepal. During Shrawan, some people fasted on every Monday while others refrained from non-vegetarian food throughout the month. Then there were some who became teetotallers to please Lord Shiva, the favourite god in this country of Pashupatinath. But the fasting in Bhadra was even more intense. On Teej—a Hindu festival that falls in the second half of Bhadra—many Hindu women observed fast for more than 24 hours, without consuming even a drop of water. I have never been much of a faster, and feats like these seem herculean to me. That is probably why I was stunned when I heard about Charles Sobhraj's plan to fast.

Of course, a lot of people were fasting just then—many Hindu women, some of my friends, even Dr Govinda K.C., a Satyagrahi. Govinda had vowed to fast until death if the government did not fulfil his demands. There was nothing unreasonable about his demands—affordable medical education, strict inspection in medical colleges, a streamlined appointment system in medical institutions. But this was more than a new political party—Karl Marx—could approve of. The capitalistic cronies kept defaming Govinda and calling him 'mad'. This was in Nepal, a socialistic country, at least as per its constitution.

Charles Sobhraj, perhaps, couldn't stand being out of the news. He decided to start a fast too—a fast until his death, much like Govinda.

'I am going to start a fast to death. Can my heart tolerate that?' he inquired during a visit.

'Are you insane? Why do you want to fast?'

'For justice! They have been cancelling my hearing for almost two years. It didn't happen last Sunday either. I refuse to tolerate this anymore.' He crumpled some papers on the desk in agitation. I removed them quickly, lest he destroyed important medical documents.

'Look, Charles. Do not fast. Your medication can get affected if you do.'

Whether it was my warning that changed his mind or he simply chickened out, I cannot say. But when I asked him about it in the next visit, he gave me a curious response.

'I did fast, and yet, I didn't.'

'What does that mean?'

'So, I tried to fast for a while, but it made me feel too weak. So, I convinced the jailer and other security guys to inform the media and the Supreme Court that I was fasting.'

I shook my head in disapproval but did not comment.

'By the way, doctor saab,' Charles leaned forward and whispered, 'Reik is in town. He wants to meet you.'

'Okay. You can give him my phone number.'

Charles looked puzzled. 'But I don't have your number. You refused to give it to me when I asked you.'

Oh, right. I sometimes withheld my personal mobile number from patients and their relatives. I may be a doctor, but the hospital was hardly a charitable one. No one paid my phone bills or gave me any incentives for being in incessant contact with my patients, even if they rang me up at 3:00 a.m., complaining of a toothache or heartburn. I had tried to be continually available at one point in my career, but it had almost killed me. My phone kept vibrating in the middle of a movie, in the middle of dinner, when I brushed my teeth. I had once calculated that I operated on nearly 700 patients in a year. If everyone wanted to call me to check something or the other, that averaged to about two calls every night for the first year, four by the second year...pretty soon, I would be up all night talking on the phone!

I cautiously gave my phone number to Charles, requesting him not to share it with anyone but the Reik guy.

As my luck would have it, Reik rang bang in the middle of a movie—*Bahubali 2*—only a day after I had shared my number with Sobhraj. It was a policeman who called me first, taking me completely by surprise as I sat in the theatre, immersed in the action of the movie. It struck me then—all the policemen knew about Reik too.

'I am calling to fix a venue for our meeting, doctor,' Reik whispered to me over the phone. If everyone in the jail knew about Reik and was actually facilitating this conversation, then why was the hush-hush necessary?

'I can meet you at Hotel Shambala at six in the evening.'

Drat it. I really hated how intrusive mobile phones could sometimes be!

★

At the restaurant that evening, Reik sat across the table with a rather fat man beside him. Both had arrived on time. Unlike his companion, Reik looked lean and fit, his energy resembling that of some journalists I had seen on television.

'Doctor, we need to shoot an interview with Charles. He will ask the questions,' Reik began, pointing towards his companion.

'I am a criminal psychologist,' said the fat man. Reik did not bother to introduce him to me. 'I have frequently worked with Scotland Yard. I need to ask Sobhraj something.'

These guys were after a scandalous television programme, a tête-à-tête with the convict. They were not trying to find justice for Charles, he was just deluding himself. The whole thing was so clichéd that I was almost bored. Also, I had no idea what they wanted from me.

'You can visit him in the Central Jail and ask him whatever you want. I am sure he will be willing to answer.'

'We have tried. But even the home minister has refused to help. We desperately need a psychological interview for the documentary we are making. You know, we are trying to crack open his brain and see *what* is inside, what makes him the man he is.'

I remembered the umpteen times Charles had talked about Reik. Reik, the British man who would come to help him. The friend who would come to rescue him in Nepal, travelling all the way from London. This man sitting in front of me and talking about cracked brains did not sound like that Reik at all.

'Are you his friend?' I asked Reik.

'How can anyone possibly be friends with a psychopath?'

I had no response to that. I focused on my bottle of Carlsberg, wondering when they would come to the point and tell me what I could do for them.

'So, doctor? What do you say? Could you please arrange a half-an-hour interview in your clinic? We know he is scheduled for next Tuesday.'

Ah, so this was it. Reik seemed to know everything about the hospital. Not that I was surprised, really, for I had seen money achieve far more.

'As a token of thanks,' he went on, 'we would like to arrange for you and your family a trip to England. You know, it is a very beautiful country.'

'I have already been to London. I'm not interested.' The whole plan was sick, trying to milk a doctor's visit to shoot a bitter documentary.

'Okay, never mind, we can arrange for anywhere else you want. We have a budget of five thousand euros.'

'I will not let you film anything inside my cabin. That is that, and please don't offer me more trips around the world.'

The fat man pitched in. By now, I knew he was called David. 'Forget the interview, why don't you have a video conference with us over Skype?'

'No.'

'What about your mobile phone? I think we can squeeze up to 10,000 euros if you ask the questions we provide and shoot his responses on your mobile.'

'No.'

'Doctor, you're foolish. This man is a unique psychopath, a

great subject for study in criminal psychology. Your government should formulate a plan to study such a character in captivity!'

He made Charles sound like an animal in a zoo, kept in an enclosure for everyone to look at and 'study'.

'Let me give you one piece of advice,' I said to both of them. 'Make this offer to one of the policemen who accompany Charles on his hospital visits. They often have to wait for hours and might be willing to take you up on your disgusting offer.'

I stormed out of the hotel. I don't regret not paying my share of the bill one bit.

*

It was Tuesday, the day of Charles's next visit. He was sitting on the same chair, he always sat on the second one from the door. I was suddenly reminded of a friend of mine from college, who had a particular urinal he always peed in.

'Doctor, is your consent form ready?'

It was. I handed it to him, and he started reading every word, voicing some of the text out loud.

'Just sign,' interrupted Shakuntala. She accompanied him on most of his visits. 'There is no need to read every word. Bhanja is not among those who want to prolong your imprisonment.'

'Did you meet Reik and the lawyers?' Charles asked me as he handed back the signed copy of the consent. 'What did they say?'

His voice was heavy with anticipation, and I had absolutely nothing to tell him. 'Yes, I met them. They were talking about their meeting with the home minister and a judge of the Supreme Court. I just updated them on your health. You know, all these legal labyrinths are not my cup of tea.'

If Charles was disappointed, he did not express it. He started talking about his medication instead. 'Doctor, last week, I felt some discomfort, so I stopped the aspirin and had an extra tablet of Warfarin. Is that okay?'

I disliked it immensely when people self-medicated. He may be an expert in committing crimes or even criminal law, he was certainly not a doctor. 'You might have bled to death,' I told him flatly.

'Sorry!' he said, sounding anything but apologetic. 'And guess what,' he chirped on, 'I am doing my regular exercises now. I feel like I never had a heart surgery! I have even started my Karate practice.'

'Good to know.' I hadn't recommended him to start exercises yet. Certainly not karate. But this man knew it all, he did not need a heart surgeon. He needed someone else altogether.

'Next Sunday will be my last hearing, and I will be released in a month.' It was back, the perpetual refrain which had not fructified in a month of Sundays. 'I will live a normal life after that. I will write to you from France.'

His high hopes were so misplaced I hadn't a clue how to react. What was normal life? Practising martial arts in the Golghar of the Central Jail? How could he be so confident that people were working hard to set him free, that the universe was conspiring to release him from jail when it was clearly the opposite?

'Charles, have you read Greek mythology?'

That silenced him for a moment. 'Why do you ask?'

'I have a story for you that might help with the book you are planning to write. There was once a hunter in Boeotia who was renowned for his beauty. He was the son of Cephissus, the River God, and the nymph, Liriope. One day, while he was walking in the woods, a mountain nymph called Echo saw him and fell deeply in love with him. She started following him everywhere.

'One day, he sensed he was being followed and shouted, "Who's there?" Echo repeated, "Who's there?" Eventually, she revealed her identity and attempted to embrace him, but he stepped back and rudely asked her to leave. She was heartbroken and spent the rest of her life alone in the lonely valleys until nothing but an echo of her remained.

'Then, one day, Nemesis, the goddess of revenge, learned of this story and decided to punish the vain man who had so mercilessly broken a girl's heart. She lured him to a pool where he saw his reflection. Unable to realize that it was merely an image, he instantly fell in love with it. For days on end, he was unable to leave the riverside, the beauty of his reflection captivated him so much that he sat there staring at it until his death.'

'I know this story,' Charles said to me.

'Then you probably know the man's name too. He was called Narcissus.'

'So?'

'So, there's a pathological condition named after him. It's called narcissism. I think you suffer from it. I'd recommend you to consult a good psychiatrist. It would be good for you as well as for the mankind.'

He did not look at me or make any more conversation for the duration of the visit. I realized I had rudely burst his bubble of euphoria, the euphoria which led him to believe that he was a good man, fitter every second. That everything that happened in the world revolved around him. For, perhaps the very first time since I had met Charles, I had offended him. In medical terminology, I did a narcissistic abuse.

That was my last meeting with Charles Sobhraj.

18

FINAL DAYS

Back in the 1960s, a Parisian prison volunteer asked Charles, 'Why did you steal a car?'

'I stole it because I needed to,' Charles replied. 'The authorities had ordered me out of France, and I had no money. I needed a car to drive across the border.'

'Why didn't you take up a job, do some work to earn the fare for a ride?'

'Without legal documents?' he scowled. 'Yes, I tried that. I peeled dozens of potatoes for four francs an hour.'

'You know, yours is a very interesting situation,' the prison volunteer said with a slight grin. 'A man without a nationality. It intrigues me.'

—Richard Neville,
The Life and Crimes of Charles Sobhraj

We left for our big trek on a bright and sunny morning. We had planned to ride in a microbus up to Besisahar—the gateway to the Annapurna Circuit—and embark on the trail to the great Himalayas from there. Our trail would pass through the Thorang-La, 5,416 metres, and branch off briefly to Tilicho, 4,990 metres—the highest lake of its size.

'Goodbye, Kathmandu,' I waved to the hippie valley as we set off on our path from Besisahar.

'Are you ready to tell us now?' Subry asked me, tightening the straps of his rucksack around his shoulders.

For the last few weeks, I had avoided talking about Charles; my friends had noticed I was rather withdrawn, lost in my thoughts. Ever since Charles had driven away from the hospital on the day of his discharge, and after my last meeting with him when I told him the story of Narcissus, I had struggled to form my judgement. Had I treated a monster? Or had I treated a man who had become a monster partially because everyone *believed* he was one? Now, away from Kathmandu, surrounded by open valleys, I felt freer than I had done in a while. I felt ready to tell them the conclusion I had arrived at.

'Do you remember that kid we met at Jhingrana?' I asked the group. 'The one with the dragonfly?'

'Of course,' said Comrade, grimacing as he replied.

'His strings were tied around my Hilux for almost a week,' added Subry.

'I have been thinking about him. You know, every toddler is a scientist, a lover of experimentation. They want to know what would happen if they chopped an earthworm in two or drowned a puppy in a bucket of water. In a way, every toddler is a sadist too—someone devoid of sympathy. All they have at that point in life is apathy. Anyway, that is what science says.'

I saw the group listening to me intently, some of them probably wondering why I was talking about children. I went on, 'Imagine what would happen if this impressionable, underdeveloped mind goes through mental trauma. A family dispute, a turbulent childhood...the mind may then never learn to harbour empathy at all. Psychiatrists believe that it is minds like these that grow to kill, people like these who become psychopaths and serial killers. Who can tell, perhaps one day that kid may become the beast of the Khaptad trail?'

We were heading to Chame by now, at 2,670 metres above the sea level. It was to be our halt for the first night. The route was picturesque, giant waterfalls, springs and rivers dotted the landscape, forming an almost too-beautiful-to-behold backdrop to our conversations about a cold-blooded murder.

'So, you think Charles's troubled childhood turned him into such a monster?' Comrade asked, his eyes big and scared. 'Boy, that is a frightening thought!'

'I think it played a big role, but it wasn't only that. Tell me, what do most people value the most? Their name, their nationality, their association to a place they can call their own, right? I don't know how I would feel if I woke up one day and found all that stripped away from me. But for Charles, this kind of identity loss was his life.'

I remembered distinctly the documentaries I had seen about Charles's childhood, the loving way in which he had described the lychees—his favourite fruit—in Vietnam.

'Charles was brought up as a stateless child, his parents dragging him from one place to another. No one knows if he had a French passport until 1996. He was denied a Vietnamese passport, an Indian one... The French passport he finally got was also the result of a rather shrewd bargain that India made with France. What could be the best plan to earn freedom and control? Stealing! Find people gullible enough to be cheated, steal their passport, and kill them to keep things quiet.'

'Yeah,' said Subry, quietly, 'almost like a business transaction where the winner takes all.'

'Correct. Since his mind had never learned to empathize, I doubt these deeds ever evoked any guilt or sorrow in him. His focus was on carving an identity for himself, which all the passport forgery let him do. Killing, for him, was almost trivial, something that had to be done on the side.'

No one spoke about Charles any more that first night. We sat by the fire in our hotel, thinking about the people Sobhraj had murdered and burnt. I wondered if he used to stand on the sidelines, watching the people burning. Perhaps he relished how their identity burnt too, leaving behind something that was newer, brighter and shinier in the afterglow of the fire— Charles Sobhraj's new identity.

★

We left our jeep at Upper Pisang, 3,300 metres, and started on foot towards Ghyaru, 3,670 metres. Rajeev, a new member of our trekking group, had an upset stomach, and we proceeded rather haltingly. A lunch of garlic noodle soup and yak cheese seemed to help things a bit, and we speeded up after the meal. We walked along the banks of the Marsyangdi River, the snow-clad Annapurna on our left, forbidding yet majestic. By dinner time, all of us were exhausted from the day's trek. We wanted nothing but to savour the goat that Chheten Dai had arranged for us, complimented by endless glasses of local wine and an entire chocolate cake from his bakery in Mugje. And, of course, talk about the man who lurked mysteriously in our midst.

'Why do you think he targeted the hippies?' Rajeev wondered out loud, now quite recovered from his upset stomach. 'I mean, he must have become pretty accustomed to robbing rich tourists in France, no?'

'Well, robbing hippies must have been a great deal easier.' Comrade held up his glass and continued, 'Plus, he harboured quite a hatred for them. He has told the police multiple times that he hated hippies.'

'But why? What did the hippies ever do to him?'

'They represented everything he had never had,' I found myself saying, Charles Sobhraj's stories of his homeland and his pathetic, desperate pleas to save his life flashing in front of my eyes. 'He had a tumultuous childhood and miserable adolescence, always living hand to mouth, always in search of money. And here were careless hippies, travelling the world, happy with only weed and hash, living life as they pleased. I think he must have felt an extreme surge of rage whenever he met hippies. Frightening and killing them was perhaps the closest he could get to revenge. Besides, they were the easiest to steal their identities from, and even the police did not care about them.'

We left Chheten Dai's resort early the next morning and continued our trek. The golden yellow peaks of the Annapurna III now felt so close, we could almost touch them. A part of me wanted to sit by the window of my room, savouring the beauty of the peaks for a long period of time. I now knew why Chheten Dai, a heart patient with two mechanical valves inside his body, wanted to stay here, even though his sons kept insisting he shut down the hotel. He could endure a monthly ride to Kathmandu for his blood tests—a ride that took two days and involved meandering, scary roads—but he could not uproot himself from the serenity and find peace in the city.

We reached Manang in a couple of hours and continued onwards along the Tilicho trail. At the Hotel Tilicho Base Camp, 4,150 metres, we drank beer and celebrated the mini-milestone. Some of us had never ascended beyond 4,000 metres before.

'Tell us about this Knippenberg guy,' said Subry, wiping his mouth after his second glass of beer. 'Why was he so interested in bringing down Sobhraj?'

'I think Herman Knippenberg started tracking Sobhraj so vigilantly after the murder of the Dutch couple. It seems he was the one who gathered critical evidence in connection with the murders in Thailand as well as Nepal. Murdering the Dutch couple was definitely Sobhraj's biggest mistake, he underestimated Knippenberg's commitment to tracking down the murderer who slaughtered his countrymen.'

None of us got much sleep that night. The air was thin, making breathing difficult and lying down painful. At first break of light, we decided to proceed to the Tilicho Lake, 4,990 metres. I had heard it was a stunning mountain lake with crystal clear water and dazzling, snow-covered mountains on all sides. And that's exactly what it turned out to be.

I hollered at the group to get everybody's attention, including some who were still climbing. We had left Rajeev back at the hotel, he had been too sick to continue. 'Let's take a bath in the lake!' My eyes gleamed at the thought, crazy as it sounded when said out loud.

Comrade gaped. 'Does mountain sickness make people crazy?'

'Well, I have been crazy since my childhood,' remarked Subry, 'so I am in!'

The first splash into the icy cold, a few seconds under the water so high up in the mountains, it was a rush like I had rarely experienced before. My heart was thumping wildly when I came out and dried myself with the towel I had packed in my bag. The dip had been enthralling, the rush in my veins felt exhilarating. It would be easy to get addicted to stuff like this.

My group seemed to echo my thoughts. 'That was *some* adrenaline rush!' announced Manish, his breathing rushed and voice squeaky. 'I feel dangerous!'

Adrenaline. A catecholamine generated naturally by the body in response to stressful and adventurous situations. It is adrenaline that produces the thrill you feel during paragliding or skydiving—the sweet feeling of danger.

I wondered briefly if Charles Sobhraj had a slightly altered, pathological surge of adrenaline in his body. He had charges of murder in Thailand. An ordinary criminal would have stayed as far away from Thailand as possible. But what did Charles Sobhraj do? He repeatedly flew from Kathmandu to Bangkok using fake passports and identities—yet another crime to compound the ones he had already committed. Perhaps he experienced a dizzying surge of adrenaline when he lurked about in the crime scene, successfully deceiving the police, unseen and unheard. It was an adrenaline surge that blinded his better judgement. And because Sobhraj was a narcissist, his self-absorbed mind was too busy singing its praises. It was unable to realize when the adrenaline ceased being pleasurable and started being dangerous.

I had once read a research paper by a psychologist called Sandy Hotchkiss. She had identified the seven deadly sins of narcissism. They were: shamelessness, magical thinking, arrogance, envy, entitlement, exploitation and bad boundaries. Charles Sobhraj displayed all these symptoms. He suffered from a textbook case of narcissistic personality disorder, a condition where the brain becomes possessed with megalomania, an all-consuming sense of grandeur and ultimate power. Millon, a clinical theorist, had hypothesized that pathological narcissism often develops in response to inconsistent and loveless interactions in early childhood. Narcissists then attempt to compensate for this in their adult relationships. But it is a skewed, grotesque endeavour that is ill-fated from the start. Marie Leclerc, the French-Canadian woman who was one of Sobhraj's fleeting 'love interests', described this apathy the best when she said:

'I swore to myself to try all means to make him love me, but little by little I became his slave.'

★

Our trek was about to come to an end. About time too, I figured, for it was becoming harder by the minute. On more nights than I cared to admit, I had slept fitfully, taking medication to battle high-altitude sickness. But there was one aspect of Charles Sobhraj's life, one mystery about his deeds that I still hadn't voiced out loud—his doomed visit to Nepal. After all these months, after getting the unsettling opportunity to observe Sobhraj without his tailored-for-the-camera witticisms, I now had the answer. Or, so I thought!

Away in France, Sobhraj may have been away from the clutches of the police, but he was far from content. Contrary to public belief, he didn't have money—at least, not enough to sustain his lavish lifestyle. The money that came in from interviews and photo sessions was less than public estimation slated it to be, and it didn't last long. Gambling was an inconsistent solution, a bit too dependent on Lady Luck for his liking. Sobhraj decided to come up with a new plan.

I have to make a big sensation, decided Charles, *something that will bring the media to me like bees to a honeycomb. I can then charge hefty sums of money for my story. But what can the sensation be?*

He must have sat down then and thought about his karma, his terrible deeds against fellow human beings. For him returning to a crime scene was always scintillating, as enthralling in real life as in spy movies. Yes, he would return to a crime scene and hang about; what could be more newsworthy yet petrifying than a criminal on the loose, lurking about unfettered, too close yet impossible to restrain? Though there were no active cases in Thailand, he decided to refrain from going there; getting caught there could mean a death penalty and nothing else. India didn't have any case against him at all. He had already tried Afghanistan, and no one had stirred. It would have to be Nepal. Nepal would sit up and take notice and bring him back in the limelight.

'So, are you saying he *wanted* to be found in Nepal? That he did it all on purpose?' Subry asked me, sounding shocked.

'Yes. Narcissists need attention—it fuels them and helps them thrive. In fact, I strongly believe that the 'anonymous' person who tipped the media about Sobhraj's presence in Nepal was not Knippenberg. It was not a random passer-by. Journalists don't usually spend three days at a location unless someone has given them concrete evidence. I believe that someone was Sobhraj himself. He tipped *The Himalayan Times* about his whereabouts because he wanted his pictures to be in the newspapers.'

'He did get attention,' said Comrade. 'But he also ended up getting a life sentence. Doesn't sound so smart to me.'

'Don't forget Sobhraj is only human,' I declared, to a few shocked protests. 'Yes, for all the inhuman acts he has committed, I have seen his beating heart and his very human body. Like any of us, he too can—and did—make an error in judgement. He surmised that an arrest, a short trial, and eventual release from prison in Nepal would do well for his celebrity status. Throw him back into the thick of things. But I'd say this was the second biggest blunder of his life, after killing the Dutch couple.'

'You can't blame the man, really,' commented Subry. 'After all, he was convinced that the Nepalese police had nothing against him. No photographs, no evidence from back in 1975. He had no trouble getting a tourist visa. He had complete support from the embassy. There would always be someone, he thought, he could bribe if anything went awry. Probably, he was arrogant enough to think that money cannot bribe only the one who writes your destiny.'

*

A steep descend of nearly 2,000 metres brought us to the foothill of Muktinath, a serene temple equally popular among the Buddhists and Hindus.

'Dai,' Subry wanted to say something.

I bisected, 'Look! This is Muktinath, a temple where devotees confess their wrong deeds. I solemnly touched my earlobes in front of Lord Vishnu and uttered some words. Did I confess? I don't know. Did I wash my sins under those hundred eight spouts? I don't know. But I felt a new and rather energetic Raamesh inside me.'

'It was not for that, Dai,' he stopped me, 'Even Indian Premier has a plan to pay a visit here. Forget about sins and deeds. Upcoming elections are more important. Think big, Dai!'

And I thought about the big picture.

*

We were at the Fishtail Hotel in Pokhara, a restful place built on one of the peninsulas of Fewa Lake, a beautiful freshwater lake in the south of the Pokhara valley in Nepal. It was here that Dev saab had completed the first draft of 'Hare Rama Hare Krishna', his famous hippie saga. The last few days of the trek had been more gruelling than most of us had signed up for, and we had taken a flight here from Jomsom airport. I badly needed to breathe in huge gusts of oxygenated air, catch up on sleep, and train my mind not to obsess over the thoughts that went on in Charles Sobhraj's mind.

He would probably be sitting in his cell, his ears burning from all the conversations we were having about him. He had thought he was superior to everyone else, he probably still did. I wondered if he ever reminisced about his deeds. Perhaps he did, recollecting them all in glowing terms—with changing identities as easily as he changed clothes at bedtime, seducing women with his attractive looks and killing them without being caught, escaping like lightning.

Charles Sobhraj had thought he was next only to god, that he was god himself. He had assumed the right to decide who was good enough to live and who deserved to have his breath stopped in the middle of life. After all, as Charles Sobhraj supposedly confessed, he 'never killed good people'.

The sky had turned a deep shade of blue, it would soon be too dark to spot a prowler lurking in the courtyard of the hotel. A pungent smell of hash came in from the next room, disturbing yet intoxicating at the same time.

'Don't forget to shut the window,' I warned Babaji before I went back to my room and turned on all the lights.

★

By next morning, I had completed the first draft of *Charles Sobhraj: Inside the Heart of the Bikini Killer*. Writing about my experiences had been therapeutic; if nothing else, it had helped me understand the man behind the monster, the man I was, the thin line that keeps most of us sane and stops us from giving in to primal instincts. Subry was lurking behind my writing table, looking over my shoulder with a puzzled expression.

'Dai, I have been thinking about everything you've told us. There is one thing about Sobhraj that I still don't understand.'

'What?'

'You told me that the bikini-clad girl was his second victim. Then who the hell was his first victim? Did anyone ever account for that dead man or woman?'

I shut down the notebook I had been working on. The day outside was sunny—with the kind of sunlight that usually filled my heart with delight—but something damp and dark suppressed my spirits. 'Subry, do you remember how I told you about Charles's extensive travels around the world before that series of murders in the late '70s? How he travelled to Greece, Afghanistan, Iran, Turkey, Pakistan and India?'

Subry nodded. 'Yes, the bastard was quite the globetrotter.'

'Yes. He was in Thailand, living in a rented apartment, before the murder of the American girl, Teresa Knowlton. How do you think he managed all that? He must have needed an identity for international travel and lodging.'

'More forged passports?' Subry scratched his forehead. 'France had denied him a passport, so I am guessing that was his only option.'

'Yes, Sobhraj committed another forgery—an important one for him, but obviously an inconsequential one for the world. No one noticed the disappearance; no one came forward to make any enquiries. The very thought of the poor man lying dead in a deep pit creeps me out.'

'Who was he?'

'You must have heard of him. Charles even made visiting cards in his name in Thailand.'

Subry did not respond, but I could see his face turn white.

'It was Alain Gauthier.'

★

Psychopaths live among us, going about life unnoticed and appearing no different from the rest. Psychopaths are human beings with beating—if sometimes ailing—hearts, and have existed since the beginning of time. While some kill for hatred, others kill for love. Anger, frustration, revenge—there is no dearth of 'human' emotions that drive psychopaths and convince their sick minds that inhuman behaviour is justified, that killing is the only natural thing to do.

But Charles Sobhraj will always remain the one psychopath I know who killed without a motive, without a reason that even a seasoned murderer would be able to justify as adequate. Apparently, he only killed for passports and pennies, for a free licence to move around the world and sustain a lavish lifestyle that he felt suited his next-only-to-god persona. It was incredibly fun for him to silence a spate of screaming human beings, just like struggling dragonflies, and take off on international trips with new passports and new identities each time. What a gruesomely perfect way to reinvent your life with every trip!

Back home from the trek, I was posting pictures on my Facebook account when I had my nightmare one more time. Maybe for the last time! It seemed that I came across a post from my new Facebook friend. The 'monster' typed updates on social media as normally as the next guy, his fingers pushing down letters as easily as they had suffocated people to their deaths. He had posted a happy photograph in the backdrop of Tribhuvan International Airport. 'Excited to visit my daughter'—the picture was captioned. Charles Sobhraj and his 'young' wife were off to the USA, presumably on a 'pram visa' to sing lullabies to their grandchildren.

> *When I was just a little girl,*
> *I asked my mother, what will I be?*
> *Will I be pretty? Will I be rich?*

I wondered what Sobhraj's grandchildren would think of their granddad when they were old enough to understand the ways of the world. *Que Sera Sera, whatever will be, will be, the future is not ours to see.* Something told me I would soon see another post from the doting granddad, singing softly to his granddaughter in some corner of the world as it rained quietly outside.

19

THE REDEMPTION OF THE HIPPIE TRAIL

'I hate hippies. They want to save the Earth, but all they do is smoke pot and smell bad.'

—Eric Cartman, from *South Park*.

Many states of the USA and Australia have legalized marijuana. This is one recurring story that keeps propping up in the Nepalese media, subtly pressuring the government to legalize it in this country too. Every fortnight, I see interviews with professors of Ayurveda, all of them advocating the medicinal values of marijuana. Botanists share interesting facts about highland weeds and their exotic scientific names—cannabis sativa, cannabis landraces, cannabis indica, cannabis nepalese dragon.

I had a classmate, called Sohanlal, back in school. Right after Dashain and Diwali every year, I often saw him running through his father's farm, wearing nothing but thin underpants.

'Don't do that! Don't fall!' his father would shout even as Sohanlal ran through the thick bushes of 'sacred' crops, hidden from the world by a vast maize field.

It would be half an hour before his father managed to catch hold of him and gape at the resins that had stuck to his skin. 'It is expensive, do you know that?' his father would say as he used a butter knife to remove the resins. 'The hippies love it. But you're not to steal it unless you want to get a whipping! The police will catch you even if I don't!'

Sohanlal and I would chuckle after the scolding. Surely, his father was exaggerating. Why should a harmless-looking crop be illegal? Crops weren't illegal! Neither of us knew about the product or its effects, but we did know that people were willing to exchange it for coins. And coins could buy *samosas* and marbles!

My life has completed a full circle since then. It seems now that Nepal may legalize marijuana in no time. Once the grass becomes legal, no father will complain about a naked boy running across the grasslands. Fields will flourish with the magical crop, not hidden from the public eye anymore. Young boys with dragonflies will abound, begging tourists to part with money or withstand the sight of a dying dragonfly.

If that happens, a new breed of hippies, flocking to the streets of Kathmandu for hash and marijuana, will find that not much has changed in Kathmandu since the time Charles Sobhraj ruthlessly haunted its streets. Their microbus can bring them through the 'overland trail', which appears quite functional and thriving, recently tested by the outgoing German ambassador. Jhonchhe will still be called Freak Street and the Monkey Temple, still a popular habitat for primates.

Yet, I don't know if the hippie trail will ever get revamped. If carefree, spirited hippies will once again backpack across the villages and towns of Nepal, seeking freedom from the clutches of the materialistic world.

Perhaps, it won't happen as long as the beast of the hippie trail is alive—an old, toothless but breathing monster in the Central Jail of Nepal.

Perhaps, it won't happen as long as the fear of the beast lives on in stories and fables, passed on from the silent peaks of the Annapurna to the whispering winds that blow along the hippie trail.

DISCLAIMER

I was chosen to operate on the ailing heart of Charles Sobhraj, a renowned, ruthless, serial killer from the hippie era. Initially, I was cautious, albeit a little thrilled. But as time passed by, I found curiosity and a deep sense of unsettlement take over me. I felt compelled to try to solve the puzzle that the man was, the puzzle that his dire deeds were.

During his hospital stay or regular follow-ups, he never showed any sign of guilt or remorse. He remained hopeful and buoyant throughout, always telling me about his 'next-day release' or the prosperous, celebrity life awaiting him outside prison. His words always reeked of a superiority complex, a feeling of being better and deserving better than everyone around. His behaviour fell way outside the normal distribution of the human population, compelling me to study him. In this book, I have tried to put together all the cards surrounding his personality and character and tried to analyse them in light of the life that he has lived. Keeping within my medical ethics, I found that my study helped me a great deal in unfolding the skewed functioning of this brutal brain.

I believe that Charles Sobhraj has a unique, but disturbed, mind and that a detailed medico-psychiatric study on him will reveal something new, strange and fruitful for criminal psychology.

Since Charles Sobhraj was a proven murderer in my country, I possessed the right to talk about him, write about him, and discuss his character, even without taking his consent. His court hearings and other documents were freely available for public reference in Nepal. However, tempting as it was during my numerous meetings with Charles, I refrained from asking him about his identity or enquiring about his past deeds.

ACKNOWLEDGEMENTS

My knowledge of Charles Sobhraj was enriched by the research work of many journalists, scholars of criminology, psychology, and human behaviour. Chapters six and eight were written entirely from my review of previously published documentaries, books and articles on Charles Sobhraj. These included *The Life and Crimes of Charles Sobhraj* by Richard Neville and Julie Clarke, and *Crime and Punishment of Charles Sobhraj* by Ananta Raj Luitel and Bikash Bhattarai. I have taken the liberty to generously quote excerpts from their work in this book. I have also referred to documentaries made by Interpol and various other producers, and interviews conducted by Tim McGirk, Tom Vater and Andrew Anthony. I am deeply indebted to all of them.

I would also like to thank Shambu Sahu, my editor, for his support in helping me complete this book. We read many books by European writers, writing in non-English languages, whose works have been translated into English and are reaching worldwide audiences. But here in South Asia, many authors are unable to cross geographical boundaries. I was fortunate to find an editor like him who helped me cross this barrier and keep me motivated throughout. Indeed, there were times when I was ready to return the signing amount and declare myself a failed author, but he showed faith in me. He kept up both the encouragement and the persistent phone calls. Apart from him, my editor, Nishtha Kapil, and managing editor, Elina Majumdar, have turned a raw manuscript into a readable book. Thank you all!

I would like to sincerely honour late Sanjay Neupane for literally dragging me to the world of writing. People say it takes an entire university to raise a writer. I don't know whether Kedar Sharma should be the chancellor of my hypothetical alma mater or Jugal Bhurtel. Dean Subhash Adhikary always marked my assignments fairly. Other faculty members were Anil Acharya, Barna Neupane, Aditi Adhikari and Durga Karki. My sincere gratitude towards my mentors who painstakingly read, rewrote wherever needed, and fulfilled the umpteen requests I sent their way.

While I was writing this book, there were days and nights when I was unable to distance myself from the horror of it all—the reality of the killings, the sins a human being is capable of. At such times, my daughter, Ishita, helped me return to my safe, normal family life—the life where I was a father struggling to meet the endless demands of his doting but demanding daughter. I also owe a special thanks to my wife, Poonam, who kept me sane by being more concerned about the weekly vegetable stock than the killer haunting my laptop. She reminded me every other day that being a writer wasn't easy, and I needed to hang in there. Thanks, Ishita and Poonam!

Finally—and this one is perhaps the most important—I want to thank you, my reader, for reading this book as an honest attempt at understanding criminology and coming to terms with the dilemmas that exist in a doctor's life. There were numerous occasions when I felt confused and scared. Was I glorifying Charles Sobhraj? Was I rating his cunning and confidence over his brutality? This book is my endeavour to recount my experiences of treating this man, commonly called heartless, and discovering for myself that it isn't only a beating heart that makes someone human. Thank you, readers, for being a part of this journey.